To my children

Acknowledgments

Without the inspiration of Naoko Haga and her late husband, Hiroshi, it is unlikely I would have spent this spring day as I did. I thought of them often as I wandered through the hollow recording my impressions, and to them both I extend my deepest appreciation.

I owe an equal debt of gratitude to my friend Mary LaMar. Had it not been for her encouragement and support, my notes of this day could have easily remained just that, filed, unpublished, in some attic corner.

Amy Hertz, my editor at Harper San Francisco, I thank for an insight that at times left me in awe. When she first read through the manuscript of this book, it was much like a garden. While my attention was on what I had planted and grown, hers was on the weeds. She identified them—I went in with the scythe—and the book's essence emerged, streamlined and clarified. I would also like to thank Juda Bennett and Theresa Everline for their editorial suggestions during the early stages of the manuscript's development, as well as Michael Toms of New Dimension Radio, and my good friends, Marcel Hernandez, Dave Haenke, and Ronald Ross, all of whom took the time to read through it, sharing their thoughts, impressions, and refreshing objectivity.

I am also deeply grateful to my mother-in-law, Verna Morrell, both for reminding me to eat on occasions when absorption in my work had caused me to forget, and for spending over a decade now boldly rearranging bookstore shelves to display my titles to advantage. I also wish to thank my oldest daughter, now Valarie Rinko, for devoting a month of her time

to various ways in which the book might be illus-
trated; and my agent, Katinka Matson, for interesting Harper San Francisco in the project and sharing
her enthusiasm for it at a time when my own was lost
beneath an avalanche of detail.

Tangibly, spiritually, practically, many have con-
tributed in some way to the process of bringing this
book into form. Stuart Bradley, Sybil Babington,
Ken and Leah Dick, Oscar Motomura, Hede Marker,
Mark Courtman, Elisabeth Jones, Bob Horton—it
might have taken me months longer to complete this
project without your encouragement and support.
Paul and Peg Eiler, Dr. Ron Cole, Franca Dal Toso,
Murray and Laurie Clark, Diane Jergins, Kathy
McMillan, Darla Chadima and Geoffrey Hulin, Bryn
Schultz, Thomas Gilligan, Peter Van Dyck, Mark and
Sue Woollard—my heartfelt appreciation to each of
you.

And particular thanks to my friends Terry and
Sue Stout, Donna Martin, Dr. John Harris, Andy
Wasserman, and John Midgley—and of course my
wife, Sherry, whose willingness to spend long hours at
the keyboard and take on many of my usual responsibilities enabled me to devote the necessary time to
writing.

I would also like to thank each of you who are
mentioned in these pages. For the times we had together, and the memories we share.

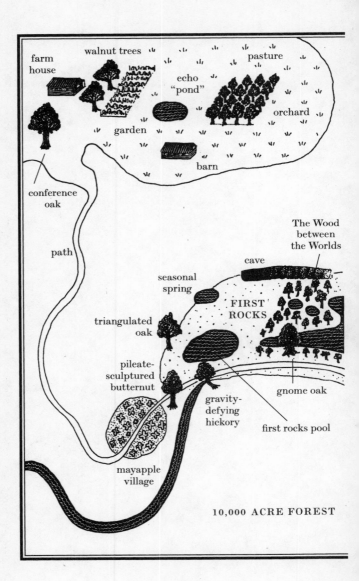

farm house

walnut trees

pasture

echo "pond"

orchard

garden

conference oak

barn

path

The Wood between the Worlds

cave

seasonal spring

FIRST ROCKS

triangulated oak

pileate-sculptured butternut

gravity-defying hickory

gnome oak

first rocks pool

mayapple village

10,000 ACRE FOREST

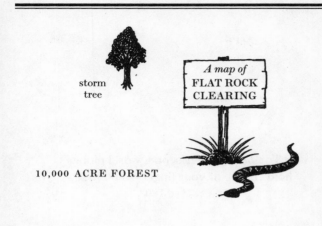

storm tree

A map of
FLAT ROCK CLEARING

10,000 ACRE FOREST

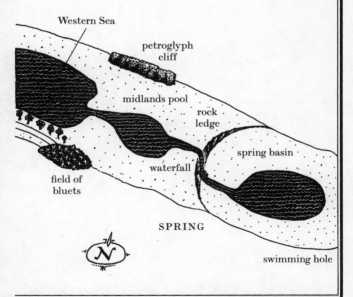

Western Sea

petroglyph cliff

midlands pool

rock ledge

spring basin

waterfall

field of bluets

SPRING

swimming hole

To find the Ozarks on a world globe,
hold the tip of your finger over Tibet,
and rotate 180°.

I AWOKE TO A ROOM filled with the light of a planting moon, low in the western sky. From a window I
watched it disappear behind a ridge of newly leafed
trees. Tonight, when I see it next, that moon will rise
full. Quietly I dress, gather up my backpack, and prepare a simple breakfast.

May. When the earth's Northern Hemisphere awakens from winter's sleep and all of nature bristles with
the energies of new life. My work has kept me indoors
for months now. I'm not sure I'll ever get used to it. Except for three years at the post office, I spent the first
half of my adult life as a carpenter, working outdoors
more often than not. Then I founded a one-room country school that soon became the focal point for an environmental initiative. We prevented the clear-cutting of
a local forest, but by then I had written a book and was
in the midst of writing another, and the bulk of my
work had shifted to the desk. Today I have other plans.

Softly I close the door behind me and step out
onto an open second-floor porch that I built without
screens or railings to provide a clear view of the horizon to the east. Cross-legged, I settle down and lean
back against the oak siding, enjoying my breakfast,
and anticipating the sunrise.

My house rests on a hilltop clearing at the end of a
dirt road in the Ozark Mountains of southern Missouri.
Surrounding it are rolling, forest-covered hills. I live

with my wife, three teenagers, and a four-year-old. The nearest town, of not quite six hundred residents, lies more than a dozen miles to the north. Working at home has advantages in such a remote location; its drawback is that I sometimes find it difficult to leave my work behind.

Over the course of a winter, choice has a tendency to degenerate into habit. By late spring my habits have usually assumed the guise of a disgruntled employer. Since this leaves me with somewhat less elbowroom than I prefer, whenever it happens, I pack a few odds and ends and strike out into the forest.

Perhaps long ago people responded to the spring as naturally as any sun-warmed seed. It may be that some still do. But for me it requires a deliberate step—a time set aside in a natural landscape, dedicated to a release of habitual thought and behavior, a time alone, in which my only goal is to move beyond the frame of my usual tasks and concerns, to rediscover who I am in nature's frame.

Half a mile away, above the oaks that rim the distant pasture, the sky shows the first hints of approaching day.

With the earth's steady roll toward the light of the star that at this proximity is a brilliant sun, the night's moisture-laden atmosphere rises coalescing, proposing rain in the morning air. One by one the morning stars fade, and the Milky Way recedes, melting into the silent beauty of the dawn. The whippoorwills become tumultuous during this hour. I hear them off in the forest—dozens by the sound—but not so near as to drown out the surrounding martin-robin-meadowlark serenade. This is the hour of singing.

While the heavens are yet full of the bolder stars, I watch the blue-green horizon floating quietly toward me. Slowly the forest emerges from darkness into a hazy, blue glow. Through a cool mist I make out the shapes of our orchard trees, the barn, the fence that runs along the garden. Sometimes I still find it hard to believe how I came to live here, surrounded by miles of forest, in mountains that are said to be among the oldest on earth. The landscape before me has little in common with the world I knew as a child. Chicago.

By the time I was tall enough to look out across it from our eighth-floor window, the trading center around old Fort Dearborn had swollen into a county of five million people; and the only sign of the fort was a brass plaque in the heart of America's second largest city.

On the site of the barn where my great-grandfather used to milk the family cow stood a weathered-brick high rise. Behind it, an alley and parking area covered the old garden spot—the soil he had worked as a boy. My great-grandmother outlived him long enough to tell me this when she was ninety-two years old and I was seven. At that time a busy intersection marked the spot where she had been born. In a farmhouse. Her earliest memories, she said, were of her mother rocking her to sleep on its front porch to the sounds of crickets, peepers, and whippoorwills.

As children, she and my great-grandfather had experienced a way of life in which it was second nature to grow your own food on the land around your home, a way of life rooted in the seasons and the soil and in the basic country values that for countless centuries had characterized every generation before them. But they were the last of my ancestors to know such a life.

The Chicago Fire brought it to an abrupt end. The old city was destroyed; and agriculture had no place in the new industrial city that rose from its ashes. Great-grandma O'Leary became a schoolteacher; my great-grandfather joined the police force. By the time I came along, that O'Leary garden soil had lain fallow since the summer of 1871, and so, too, I think, had something in my people's soul.

When you've been a couple hundred generations marking time by first and last frosts, phases of the moon, and the migratory patterns of wild geese, something in your blood gets used to that garden always being just a stone's throw from the cooking fire. When harvest time rolls around and buildings tower around you instead of trees, you may not understand what lies behind it, but you get to feeling mighty restless inside.

Within me was the passion, the love of the open country that had inspired my ancestors through all those generations before the Great Fire. I enjoyed the feel of freshly turned soil, the way it smelled, the taste of what it grew. My blood ran thick with the instincts of farmers and fishermen, hunters and gatherers, country people whose lives had centered on the land, the weather, the churning of the sea, the turning of seasons.

As a boy, I would lay in bed at night thinking of that O'Leary garden. Soon I would be walking past it with a pail of milk, pausing in my imagination to check for ripe melons or summer squash. Dinner would be simmering on the wood stove, hickory smoke drifting through the air. By and by, the cooking smells would draw me into sleep and I would drift off into dreams . . . of trout, catfish, fresh-dug potatoes, and homegrown greens.

And I'd wake up hungry.

Hungry for mountains and forests, for clear air and spring-fed creeks, for a backwoods hollow to roam and a piece of land that felt like home. As the years passed that hunger grew until there were nights in that county of five million when I felt as restless as a caged wildcat, and days when all I did was look for some chink in that twenty-seven-hundred-people-per-square-mile maze, some break in the hedge that I could squeeze through and find my way home.

So when I noticed the '55 Chevy with *$200* scrawled across its windshield, I bought it. The next day I loaded up my things and began driving west. My two-hundred-dollar investment made it all the way to the top of Mount Tamalpais before darkening the California skies with a cloud of smoking oil and vaporized engine parts.

With night falling and a thick fog billowing upward from the sea, I attempted a shortcut down the mountain, discovered Muir Woods, and got my first taste of nonindustrial time. My possessions had dwindled to a sleeping bag and the clothes upon my back, but that was true wealth, for it was all I needed.

From the Del Norte redwoods to the Sierra Madres, I explored the forests and mountains, spending my nights in the open air and forging the ties with the earth that would guide me through the years ahead. I stopped counting the days; they passed into seasons, and the seasons turned. One night in a eucalyptus grove on the Berkeley campus I met a woman whose passion to put down some country roots was as all-consuming as mine.

Within an hour we were talking of farms and gardens and the importance of children growing up in a place where they could fish and swim and explore a land whose fields were not covered with asphalt and whose streams did not flow beneath city streets. Sometime between midnight and the changing of the campus guard, we scaled a ten-foot gate and found ourselves alone, but for the light of the moon, in the eerie outdoor beauty of the Greek Theater.

Time paused. The pounding surf of measured hours relaxed into a clear, still sea. We wandered the moonlit stage and tiers of outdoor seats, sharing our hopes and dreams and forgiving the circumstances of our respective lives that had postponed our meeting until this soft November night.

She told me things about myself no one could have known but me; and in her eyes I saw leaves and trees and the bearing of a creature of the wild. It showed in her confidence, her trust in abandon, in her calm and easy control. We made love in the third row of crescent benches, and while the wind filled the air with the fragrances of eucalyptus and short-leaf pine, I proposed.

"Sherry," I asked, "would you like to come and live in the forest with me?" She answered with a heartfelt affirmative.

Side by side we put in some hardworking years, managing our money carefully, saving all we could to buy a piece of land. When the dust had settled, we were sitting on an eighty-acre farm at the end of a dirt road in a heavily forested corner of the Ozark Mountains where no humans had lived for as many years as there were leaks in the old tin roof of the house that stood in the center of our land. *Our land.* How good it felt to say it! During our first year in these mountains we felt a spirit of renewal so powerful we thought it would last forever.

Any oak in the forest could have told us we were wrong.

The first lesson nature taught us is that only the dying rest on last season's laurels. If our lives were to be more than mere human impositions on the land

and to evolve—as we hoped they would—into human expressions of the land, we had to open our minds and hearts to the renewing energies of spring. And not just once, but every spring. Like the trees, we had to let each new year shape, teach, and renew us until our unconscious habits fell like autumn leaves to the forest floor, and new, more conscious ways of doing things sprouted in their place.

And so it happened that we began a tradition.

Every year, on certain mornings in April or in early May, one or the other of us will throw a few things in a backpack and set out to enjoy a day in the forest. A quiet rest in the shade of a tree may lead to a memory that at first seems random, yet in the flow of recollection the solution to a problem may appear, a decision may be made, or an opportunity recognized. Appreciation of the natural world draws out a self within us that knows what we, in our busyness, often forget.

I remember things in the forest, things I never intended to forget. Things that, as a child, I would not have believed could be forgotten. Johnny, our four-year-old, sometimes tells me of having seen faces in doorknobs or of hearing voices among the trees—as if he senses some dimension within and behind what is culturally seen, an *alam al mithal*, as the Sufis say, where awareness saturates every particle, and beings inhabit all things.

Outdoors, immersed in nature's season of renewal, there are moments, I find, when such perception comes. Moments when my awareness recognizes itself in all I see, and every pebble and leaf and tree looks back at me, mirroring some facet of myself.

When I feel I have been too long without this awareness, I know it is time once more to strike out

alone into the forest, to experience a day among animals, trees, and open sky.

I awoke knowing this was to be such a day.

High above I watch the last deep purple of night
tumble into a blanket of color that transmutes it into
ever-lighter shades of blue. In the garden below, a
flock of robins effectively combs the strawberry bed,
marching in methodical rows, each hopping a few
steps forward, eating, waiting for the others, then
moving forward again in orderly decorum. The damp
morning air drifts upward to embrace the porch, and
with it comes the smell of fresh-cut hay, the scents of
wildflowers and of countless—

Coffee!

Even as my thoughts about-face to trace the welcome fragrance to its source, the door opens and I am
greeted by Sherry's smile. She takes a seat beside me
and hands me a mug, steaming in the cool, damp air.

Our view of the morning is framed by a pair of walnut trees that grow so near to our porch that in places
we can reach out and touch their leaves. These two
trees will yield anywhere from our record year of 455
pounds of hulled walnuts to a poor year of only a couple hundred pounds. They are the last trees to agree
that summer has come and the first to shed their
leaves at even a hint of frost. Today they are in full
blossom, with long, slender clusters of tiny grapelike
flowers adorning their branches.

Below the walnut trees, spreading out over a quarter acre, our upper garden is dressed in a coat of dandelions whose flowers have given way to fluffy halos
of tiny parachute-equipped seeds. The children call
them wishing flowers, believing that if you make a
wish and succeed in blowing all the fluffy seed pods
into the wind, your wish will come true.

This morning my only wish is that every child here in Shannon County wakes up as happy as these dandelions—of which there are probably about as many scattered throughout this field as there are children in this remote Missouri county. Sherry says there's a good chance my wish will come true. Today is the last day of school.

A female martin flutters to rest on a twig of the southernmost walnut tree. Between bites of its drooping, catkin flowers, she releases a melodic warbling call. From a distant grove of trees comes the muffled drumming of a pileated woodpecker who, from the sound, is probably rounding off breakfast with the contents of a log in spongy-soft decay.

Beyond the garden fence, in the pasture just this side of the orchard, Sherry points out the bobbing heads of several wild turkeys. In the orchard a doe winds her way among the apple blossoms, starts momentarily at the cawing of a crow, wags her tail, and continues grazing.

Suddenly a hush falls over the bird world. The happy cacophony of chirps and warbles ceases until the only sound is the solitary lowing of a distant cow. For a timeless breath, all of nature waits. Then it comes, breaking out above the treetops—the upper rim of a fiery orange sun.

A wave of golden light ripples toward us across the pasture. Everywhere it looks like tiny bulbs are being lit as each blade of grass—ornamented with grain encased in veneers of vivid crystal dew—is touched by the morning light. Smoothly, with surprising speed, the sun floats free and clears the pasture's ridge of trees. The birds resume their chirps and warbles. I shoulder my backpack, take leave of Sherry, and chart a course for the mossy hollow where I plan to spend the day.

THE PATH I FOLLOW from the house leads me down a steep hillside into a forest that extends for many thousands of acres in all directions. Journeying downward into its mist-shrouded intimacy, oaks, pines, and hickories flank my path. It gets cold on these Ozark mornings. If I didn't know this was May, the chill could convince me the leaves had just fallen.

When people tell me I am doing the best in my life, I am usually nearer my worst. When I appear the most successful, in my inner life I am often failing— or near to it. Not because my activities are inappropriate, but because their success indicates that I am at the end of a cycle of routine and now require movement into the altered perception that alone can restore my sense of balance and perspective.

My life has been a roller coaster of virtual paradise and verifiable hell. If I have acquired any wisdom along the way, it is because I have made so many mistakes. I tell myself this is not altogether bad. The burnt child shuns the fire; and the individual with a résumé of errors is bound to be a bit wiser than one who merely tiptoes through life, afraid to take chances. At least, I hope this is true.

Seven years without radio, television, or newspapers made it clear to me that until then I had been living in a world defined by values other than my own, a world of description, handed down to me by family, culture, and by the language through which I was taught to filter my impressions. Those years of isolation also showed me just how much we depend on each other, and that it is neither possible nor desirable to break the ties that bind us to society. During that same time, we also lived without plumbing and electricity, but that taught me nothing. Except that I wanted them.

Within the next quarter mile, this path will make a sharp turn toward the east and continue into the heart of a hollow carved by eons of wind and weather from the limestone deposits of an ancient sea. Along the bed of the seasonal creek that runs through the center of this hollow is a natural garden of extraordinary beauty. The area is home to a broad spectrum of herbs, wildflowers, ferns, mosses, forest creatures, and a vast array of miniature geological formations. Rolling, moss-covered stones worn by millennia of rainfall form its two open areas, both of which are flanked by ponds whose banks meet the forest in a luxuriant tangle of vegetation.

Surrounded by rocky, forest-covered hills, its many stone declivities catch the rainwater in a series of shallow pools that spill over tiny waterfalls into lower pools, then on into pools lower still. As beautiful as the most exquisite of the teahouse gardens I have visited in Japan and, for me, more inspirational and calming than even the most famed of our botanical gardens, it is an area I frequent when long hours indoors clamor for a change.

The terraced rock ledges that form the lower portion of this primitive garden end abruptly in an eight-foot drop, beneath which bubbles a crystal-clear mountain spring. During our first seven years here this spring was our only source of drinking water.

When our children were young, one five-gallon jug every second day was usually enough to meet our needs, but as our family grew, I often had to make the half-mile trip for water several times a day.

I always enjoyed those excursions for something so simple, so basic and beautiful as water. The walks through the hollow, the short waits while the jug filled, and even the long uphill trek back home provided welcome interludes of contemplation. Only after several years of drought had taken heavy tolls on our garden did we finally drill a well, which has since complemented the spring's near-central role in our lives.

Being the only year-round spring within several miles, it is the watering hole for beaver, bear, coyote, cougar, bobcat, raccoon, possum, woodchuck, and deer. Birds of nearly every description frequent it, including blue heron and wild turkey, and even the occasional unexpected visitor, like the bald eagle I once spotted there or the wood ducks that some years choose it as their nesting place.

As I reach the bottom of the hill, the path I follow toward this spring levels out along the floor of the hollow. Just north of it I notice a cluster of plants that on first glance I mistake for Queen Anne's lace, but a closer inspection of their seven dense clusters of tiny white flowers shows that they are yarrow. The tea made by steeping these flowers provides effective allergy relief, and I have probably consumed more of it than of any other tea. For years I would begin each day during the allergy season with several cups, then head off to work with my quart thermos filled with more. I took a good deal of ribbing from my fellow workers when break time rolled around. While they uncorked their thermoses and poured their coffee, I would pour myself a steaming cup of bright yellow tea with a pungent, weedy odor that quickly made the rounds.

"What'd you make that with," Clarence would ask, "grass clippings? I could make a better smelling brew with scrapings from the underside of a bush hog."

But the yarrow tea is as effective as any antihistamine and has no mind-dulling side effects. Its taste is slightly bitter, but since I drank so much of it, I refrained from adding any sweetener. Over time I grew to enjoy its wild grassy flavor. It is said that Achilles used yarrow to heal wounds; how I do not know, but it would not surprise me to learn that it also has antiseptic properties.

A tick ambling up my leg reminds me that I had best splash a little pennyroyal oil about my ankles. I don't know why more people don't use it. I have found pennyroyal not only more effective than the various chemical concoctions for warding off insects but far healthier. And the smell is pleasant. A light film on my bare feet and ankles, and just the slightest splash on the back of my neck, cause most of the insect world to mistake me for a large, repugnant herb. (I admit there is some deceit involved here, but if they knew the truth they would likely regard me as breakfast.)

The oil extracted from the leaves and flowers of the pennyroyal (or blue curl) also offers protection from gnats, blackflies, chiggers, and mosquitoes. It will keep at bay even those troublesome horseflies that I am convinced have been assigned to teach our race the dangers of extreme pacifism. On those rare occasions when the pennyroyal fails, I have no qualms about mashing the green-eyed pests—if I can move quickly enough.

Once, while I was lecturing in Japan, a Buddhist monk took issue with my less than divinely compassionate attitude. It was touch and go for a while, but I finally silenced him by pointing out that mashed mosquitoes reincarnate in forty-five seconds, horseflies in thirty seconds, and fruit flies and gnats, every five seconds.

"What about blackflies?" someone asked.

"Depends on the latitude," I said, "and on the season of the year. But in Missouri? During the summer? Seems to me they just rematerialize before your eyes."

The kill-nothing philosophy is sublime. But in the Ozarks anyone exhibiting so pacific a temperament during summer months would soon be compost. And I don't mean unappreciated compost: well used and thoroughly enjoyed.

Becoming compost is, I suppose, a noble and worthy end. I myself aspire one day to no higher an ambition. Yet even without the recent medical reports showing that the lead lining used in coffins poses serious health risks to their occupants, I still would not want my mortal remains lead-sealed in some glorified tin. It won't bother *me* if my grave is a shallow one. However, in the meantime (and I can't help but have this morning in mind) I will do my best to ensure that this aspiration for the mortal part of me is not achieved in my lifetime.

I am quite clear about this.

After twenty summers in these lively hills, my own perhaps crude and primitive opinion definitely favors the defense of my biology. Take chiggers, for example, those invisible bugs whose favorite place to deposit their larvae is beneath the skin of your ankles, stomach, and armpits—in colonies that cry punctually for feeding every half hour throughout the night. Call me inhospitable if you will, but I do not believe in feeding the local wildlife such expensive fare.

Mosquitoes I can live with, at least in the modest numbers in which they appear here. On those rare occasions when they do land on me, I usually ignore them, allowing them their place in nature's local design as I am given mine. But chiggers and ticks are a different story. They lack the manners of the civilized bugs. They do not leave after breakfast but plod on through lunch and supper, and if one is not wary, they can feast for days at your expense—or should I say expanse?

Despite the overwhelming tick population here in these wooded hills and hollows, we would often go for an entire summer without ever seeing so much as a single one of these mannerless guests. Those were summers when the land upon which we lived supplied our food (ten years in all), and I'm convinced this is the reason the insects left us alone. Since every cell in the human body replaces itself periodically, our bodies during that decade came to be made up entirely of local water and soil, making it difficult for the insects to distinguish us from the general landscape. Chemically as well as spiritually, it seems, we had blended well enough with our surroundings to obscure those odoriferous distinctions that cause them to hunger and thirst.

Our food was excellent during those years. Our diet consisted almost exclusively of what we grew in our garden. Each summer we would preserve between fifteen hundred and nineteen hundred quarts of tomatoes, carrots, green beans, spinach, zucchini, corn, beets, and other vegetables. Pickles and sauerkraut we put up in five-gallon crocks. Cheeses, made from our cow's surplus milk, we stored by the dozen in three-pound waxed rings. One year we even canned the prolific poke (*Phytolacca americana*) and wild lettuce (*Lactuca* species) against the possibility of hard times, but found that, preserved, these wild plants were not as good as more typical garden fare, although fresh and in season they are delicious.

From May to September our table was a cornucopia of nutrition and variety. In winter we enjoyed our canned vegetables and found satisfaction in the knowledge that they were grown without pesticides or chemical fertilizers. But since we had chosen to live without electricity, we were unable to freeze our surplus, and our winter's supply of dried, canned, and otherwise-preserved foods did become monotonous at times. Along about December or January, I sorely missed a fresh salad or piece of fruit—luxuries that my two-dollar-an-hour carpentry income would not allow. But I never once tired of wheat or potatoes, which even now remain the staples of our winter diet.

Whole wheat bread! Made from local Amish wheat that I earned each year in exchange for help with its harvest, baked in the oven of a wood-burning cook stove. Mondays, Wednesdays, and Saturdays I would build up my biceps hand-grinding the wheat, which Sherry or her mother, Verna, would then transform into the stuff of legend. While the loaves were still hot out of the oven, I would slice several thick slabs, lay on a quarter-inch of butter, churned from the rich yellow cream of our Guernsey cow, and sometimes top the works with a tablespoon of wildflower honey gathered from our hives. (It was not the best time to approach me, as a Jehovah Witness once did, with talk of a better hereafter.)

Potatoes were our mainstay throughout that decade, as they still are today. Usually we harvest somewhere in the vicinity of two thousand pounds, but once, due to frequent and well-timed rains, we dug and stored in our improvised back-porch root cellar nearly four tons of the delicious white-skinned Kennebecs—a record twenty-to-one yield.

Such a way of life offered us benefits far beyond a reduced cost of living and a lower profile in relation to the insects. Among them was the celebration of the firstfruits of the garden—a spiritual experience that in the procession of seasons deserves a feast day as hallowed as New Year's or Thanksgiving.

We commemorate the birth of abstractions; why not celebrate the tangible birth of the radish? Being the first of the garden's produce to delight the palate, this spicy red-and-white root would make a worthy symbol of nature's annual renewal, and of all the edible features of the new year. Often by Washington's birthday we are harvesting the first delicious mouthfuls.

Throughout February and March I carry a salt shaker in my back pocket, much to the horror of certain health-conscious neighbors. But at the risk of sounding dogmatic, I must stand up for what I believe in: *Until you have tasted a radish fresh out of the garden with a touch of salt, you have not truly lived.* You might *think* you have lived, you might *imagine* you have lived, but one who has never experienced this crisp, sensual jubilation has no right to criticize that school of thought (hedonistic though it may be) that regards a mouthful of fresh, lightly salted radish as one of the pinnacles of human experience. The salt also comes in handy for turnips, carrots, and tomatoes, although many things like asparagus, which will often tie the radish for first place in the order of fresh garden produce, are best without the addition of anything but saliva.

Facetiously I've told visiting urbanites that growing 80 percent of your own food requires 110 percent
of your time; but this is only a slight exaggeration, as
anyone who has ever made the effort knows. It would
not take this long, of course, for an adult who was
growing only enough to feed himself or herself. But
we had a family of young children who never let us
forget their need to eat. While the older ones always
helped in the garden, Sherry and I often found ourselves going for months with little or no free time.
After a decade of this, we decided to scale back.
These past few years we have grown only about 25
percent of our food. Since this only requires about 25
percent of our time, it is a far more satisfactory
arrangement.

During our first decade here a morning like today's
would have found me with little leisure. If I passed
this way at all, it would have been with five-gallon jug
in hand on a trip to the spring to fetch water for coffee and oatmeal; and as much as I enjoyed those
trips, they rarely afforded me this quality of time to
so thoroughly enjoy my surroundings.

In the distance I see the opening through the trees
where the path enters the first of several clearings of
mossy limestone from which this hollow has earned
itself the name Flat Rock. The soil that surrounds
this first of its clearings contains the typical Ozark al-
lotment of rock and gravel, yet in places where the
creek's regular flooding leaves silt deposits, the soil
can be nearly as fertile as a river bottom. A cluster of
Jerusalem artichokes on my right has apparently
found such a spot, for these plants are as nutrient
hungry as field corn and will not grow in poor soil.

Jerusalem artichokes are the only of Missouri's
wild edibles that I have successfully cultivated. Still

relatively small this early in the season, by late summer these plants here will be five or six feet tall, but in our well-manured garden I've seen them reach a height of eleven or more feet. Boiled and served in a hot butter sauce, a small bowlful of their potatolike tubers will provide nearly twelve grams of protein as well as calcium, vitamin C, and an impressive list of other nutrients. Best of all is their taste. The tubers have a wild, crisp, nutty flavor that has made them one of my favorite garden vegetables.

The only other wild edible with nutritional properties rivaling the Jerusalem artichoke is amaranth. High in protein and many essential vitamins, its leaves can be substituted in spinach recipes, and a passable bread can be baked from flour ground from its black seeds. Hardy, fast growing, and drought resistant, it requires no care or cultivation beyond initial planting, and being a perennial, it comes up of its own accord year after year.

I first heard of amaranth from an enthusiastic neighbor who described it as the perfect survival food, claiming that a family of four could subsist for decades if need be on just a quarter acre of this so-called miracle plant. After showing me the unabashedly messianic literature sent by the distributor in Arizona from whom he had ordered the rather expensive seed, he promised to share some with me when it arrived.

When presented with the seed, I followed the instructions on the packet and sowed a row of it in the garden, wanting to verify its properties before committing an entire quarter acre. I was gratified at how quickly the strange-looking seed sprouted—not a single gap in the entire hundred-foot row. And the plants! *Fast growing* was an understatement. But they looked strangely familiar. By the time they were

knee high (a mere week later), there was no longer
any doubt. I drove immediately to my benefactor's
house.

"For God's sake, Doug, it's nothing but pigweed!"

He stood there sadly surveying the quarter acre he
had laboriously cleared, tree by tree, from the forest.
He had planted it all in pigweed, the most common
and troublesome garden pest since the first Sumerian
plot—the curse of every cultivated lot. My outrage
dissolved into sympathy.

"Well, at least you won't have to weed it," I offered.

"No," he replied, "I'll burn it off before it spreads
and chokes out the oaks and hickories."

Amaranth and Jerusalem artichokes are just two
of the many wild foods that grow here. Besides the
abundant wild grapes, blackberries, huckleberries,
poke, miner's lettuce, and lamb's quarter (all of
which we have had success preserving as well as eating fresh), and not counting the native plum, pear,
pawpaw, cherry, persimmon, and indigenous black
walnut trees, I have identified over forty other common edibles growing wild in fields and along the roadsides—and probably half that many again growing
along the bottom of this hollow.

The path now opens out before me into the first of
the hollow's rocky clearings, a realm of beautiful, almost surrealistic sculptures in limestone that the children have named the First Rocks. The stones that
form the floor of this glade are covered with patches
of thick, green moss. After a rain or a heavy dew the
moss is soft and spongy and colored a brilliant emer-
ald. When dry, it becomes brittle and crunchy and
takes on a light-olive color. This morning I encounter
only the damp velvety greens, which squish beneath

my bare feet as they release their stores of morning dew to ooze upward between my toes.

In the center of this area lies a small pond, bordered on the north by multiflora roses and on the south by oaks and dogwoods. Since it has formed in a basin of stone rather than soil, except in the driest months its shallow waters are usually clean and clear—a perfect place, we discovered, for preparing our toddlers to swim in the nearby Jacks Fork River. All of them enjoyed this pond when they were young, splashing and playing in its warm shallows, but none took to its water as enthusiastically as our daughter, Jessie, or put up a greater fuss when it was time to go. A lifeguard now at the local swimming pool, she was the first of our children to be born here. I sometimes wonder if her warm-water Leboyer birth in a quiet room of the old farmhouse may have had something to do with her love of water.

Although the rocky area above the spring is larger and possesses a more spectacular type of beauty, I have always felt my deepest affinity with the quieter beauty of these First Rocks. Few problems survive a morning here, and none, a day—the genius loci being inhospitable to anything but growth.

When twenty years ago the county clerk placed my name on the title for this land, I sensed that here I could learn more than in any university. This is a school with better credentials, for here the universe itself administers, its lessons as varied and as plentiful as this hollow's forms of life.

I have tracked down many an idea in the card catalog of this moss; and in the shade of these trees, flipped through the leaves of many a sacred volume. In these forest passages the scriptures of nature can be read in their original versions, untranslated by religions, unedited, unabridged. This is the universe's

university. The voices of nature echo along its corri-
dors, and in them are truths that have inspired the
genius of every age. If you are still, you might catch
firsthand in the rustle of leaves what Shakespeare
caught as *Tongues in trees, books in the running brooks,
sermons in stone, and good in everything.*

On mornings like this, what I remember of my for-
mal schooling seems but a thin sheet of cultural
interpretation upon the surface of otherwise fluid
awareness, a crust of overliteral definition that must
melt away before I can see this forest for all it truly is.
The pool here will acquire a coating of ice during the
cooler Ozark nights, occasionally even as late as early
May. But the tadpoles do not warm sufficiently to
swirl and swim, the frogs do not plunge lustily into
their cycles of mating, the algae does not grow, nor
reeds and grass turn green until the hardness of the
surface ice relaxes again into the warm, splashing,
sensuous milieu that is the wellspring of organic life.
So, too, with the hardening of perception, that veneer
of icy preconception that so often accompanies the
mind's accumulation of facts. Mental images of trees,
birds, flowers prevent us from seeing them as they
are. Until that superficial layer is relaxed, thought
cannot flow in the associations that bring insight and
fresh perspective.

A flurry of activity draws my attention from the
pool. A young robin seems intent on distracting me
while her partner has his swim. This is an old bird
trick intended to lead potential predators away from
their nests or, as it appears in this case, her mate. But
I may be wrong. Her male counterpart seems gen-
uinely concerned.

A downy woodpecker is pestering her and chasing
her about. She in turn gives chase. Apparently their
territory is in some dispute. I am surprised to see a

nearby blue jay abstain from involvement in all this,
for jays relish an argument more than any other bird
species, excepting, of course, the crow. But the jay
takes advantage of the commotion to fly himself to
the now-vacant pool, where with obvious content he
dips his wings.

Although the sun has not yet risen high enough
above the trees for its light to reach this low-lying
pool and its adjacent world of stone, with its steady
ascent, the number of birds here has been growing. In
the space of minutes I have seen a cardinal, a blue-
bird, an indigo bunting, several canary-yellow
finches, a pair of meadowlarks, countless sparrows,
and a flash of orange that was either an oriole or a
scarlet tanager. It seems the birds favor the open
spaces around the farmhouse for their daily breakfast
convention, but as the day warms, their center of activity shifts to the relative cool of this hollow.

It takes a while to acclimatize your senses to a
place like this. Layer by onionlike layer I can feel my
mind relaxing, letting go of its knowing, its names, la-
bels, definitions. It counts for nothing to head off into
the wilderness and leave behind only the trappings of
civilization. To experience the transformative energy
of the wild places you have to be willing to leave more
than externals behind.

FAR ABOVE, A FLOCK of clouds condensing from the night's moisture is slowly building into a coalition of white-fringed, purple-bellied forms that look exquisite against the blue of morning.

Yesterday, in our lower garden, we set out tomato, squash, cucumber, melon, and pepper plants, which, after being transplanted from the cold frame, now require generous watering. Our soil is dry at the moment; we could use a good rain. I wonder if this delegation is commissioned to discuss such matters. They look to me like subordinates; I doubt they have the makings of thunderheads, but one never knows. Clouds can build in a hurry when they have a mind to. These are building even as I watch.

From beneath them, blue-white mist tumbles then curls upward into red and green, rising like the plume of a volcano belching not smoke toward heaven, but the random contents of some artist's auroral cupboard. Before the rising plume rolls inward to add to the growing mass of gray, it passes through every spectrum of the rainbow, colored like the rainbow, by sunlight, shining through billions of tiny prisms of suspended moisture.

Sunlight. At last it breaks through into the hollow. Its first rays come to rest on a butternut tree, creating around it a circle of light so inviting that I have walked across the rocks and entered it before it occurs to me that I did so without any conscious decision. Some mothlike instinct. The warmth here is a welcome contrast to the chill that still grips the surrounding area. And it looks like I'm not the only one who thinks so.

Lumbering ominously out of the forest from a dark and shadowy thicket comes a creature right out of science fiction: two black, searching eyes mounted atop a long, slender body, its barbed-tip tail arched in readiness above its back. But on this scale it inspires no terror. As it flaps its chilly wings to drag itself into the light, I welcome it. There is warmth enough here for all, little dragonfly.

For a moment the world seems to pause as a wave of silence washes its soft enchantment through the forest. I've noticed these periodic intervals of stillness before, yet I have never been able to determine what causes them. Like tides of soothing calm they come and recede throughout the day.

A breeze stirs, and the world resumes.

The expanse of sunlight slowly grows to encompass the trees nearest the butternut: a dogwood, a hickory, a cherry, a maple. From a small, illuminated circle it expands into a glowing field of warm and cheering radiance.

I think I know now why grape vines have climbed to the tops of these trees to face their heart-shaped leaves in the direction of morning.

A flash of movement draws my eye to a low, horizontal branch of a chinkapin oak. A lizard? I'll have to walk nearer to be sure. The chinkapin is a relatively small tree that bears a strong resemblance to a California madrone. Its rust-red trunk has made it one of my favorites here, for it provides a welcome splash of color in a forest where the trunks of most trees are brown or gray. Approaching slowly so as not to frighten off whatever creature caught my eye, I see that it is not one lizard, but two. Eastern collared lizards. Are they mates? I move closer to see what I can learn. But the observer affects the observed. They freeze in midmotion as at eye level I draw within inches. While one hangs suspended beneath a scaly red branch of the chinkapin, the other pauses above, both keeping me in view.

Their faces have a disturbingly intelligent look about them, and their little five-fingered hands and five-toed feet appear eerily humanoid. The male has a pastel blue-green underbelly. His upper body is a bright configuration of yellow, brown, and green stripes, covered with a liberal sprinkling of pale yellow spots. The female has a brownish body sprinkled with the same spots and highlighted by uneven stripes of brilliant day-glow orange. They are both quite large—eight or nine inches long—and each wears the distinctive black collar from which their species derives its name.

A third enters the scene. Smaller than the others, it measures only about five inches. It can only be a green anole, though I have never seen one this far north. Has global warming given it itchy feet? It is doing push-ups on the branch, watching the others, the only one of the three unaware of its human audience.

I blink, and the anole makes a sudden lunge at the male collared. Fighting, the two of them roll off the tree and hit the flat rocks below, tumbling among the moss and scattered leaves.

A land grab? It looks more like a love feud to me, though I am no expert on lizard romance and not even sure whether such disparate species mate; but if this is indeed a green anole, it belongs to the same

Iguanid family as the others. Round and round they tumble, head over heels. My impression is that this feud goes back a ways. I doubt this is the first time they have met.

As if in response to my unspoken thought, while the anole retreats to catch his breath, the collared tilts his head askance and looks up at me as if to say, "Met one anole, you met 'em all," concluding this acrid remark by spitting from a corner of his mouth a brown stream that looks like tobacco juice.

The female, who has been observing the fracas with aplomb, looks up from the panting pair to study me curiously. We make eye contact. Moments pass. She turns away just in time to see her feisty companion remounting the branch where he hunches his back and begins doing push-ups just as the anole did before it attacked.

The anole darts back up the tree. Now all three lizards face off and begin doing push-ups in earnest. The action has a hostile look to it. The smaller anole opens his mouth wide as if to say something, then appears to change his mind and accept the collared's advice, for he slowly makes his way backward down the trunk, not taking his eyes off his adversary until reaching the ground, where instead of hightailing it out of there as prudence would suggest, he casually turns and affects nonchalance.

But the male collared decides the time has come to put an end to the matter. He pursues. His mate jumps aside to let him pass. I watch to see what will happen. The anole, pretending to stalk a fly on the flat rocks below, feigns disinterest in the movement above him.

Suddenly from the higher ground of the chinkapin the collared leaps down upon the Arkansas trespasser. With a lightning aikido roll, the anole flips him away, but the rapid expansion and contraction of the smaller lizard's tiny chest shows that his victory was not easily won. He tries to catch his breath, but the attempt is cut short.

The eastern collared lizard rears up on his hind legs. Green and yellow colors flashing in the sun, he charges upright like an enraged dinosaur at the now thoroughly spooked anole. Waving his tiny fists threateningly in the air, sprinting at unbelievable speed, the collared chases the anole into the leaves beneath a shallow cave across from the chinkapin. Twenty feet. He must have covered it in under two seconds—and running on hind legs all the while!

Lizards aren't supposed to be able to do that.

My imagination runs wild as I have a sudden image of a burgeoning new Ozark sport. Eminence, Missouri. A June afternoon. Main street closed to traffic. Colorful banners and balloons flutter above the festive crowds that line the sidewalks. Venders hawk lizardibilia, as owners guide their entries into position. The last of the bets are placed. A hush falls over the crowd, gates are lifted—and the first race is on.

Yet even as I envision the Racing Lizard becoming to Shannon County what the Jumping Frog is to Calaveras, the feisty racer who inspired my vision settles quietly alongside his mate and resumes his contemplation of the day.

One thing upon which these collareds and I wholeheartedly agree: We share the same conception of a fly's ideal fate. When the female darts forward and catches one of the fat and juicy pests, I feel no remorse or sympathy. As she works her jaws and I watch the meal slide down into her belly, it seems as fitting and proper as a Buckingham tea. I find it easy to imagine her making a brief after-dinner speech—

This winged disrespecter of bodily property
has been educated here
given a decisively, yes, decisively clear
lesson on The Nature of Territory
as pertains to present company
whom he will not trouble again
*   with the same (hick) audacity.*

"Brrribbitt, grock. Hear! Hear!"
the nearby frogs and reptiles cheer.

Both of these lizards have been glancing over at
me from time to time, even more so now that the
anole is gone. Am I as interesting to them as they are
to me? I have never yet succeeded in petting one of
these quick-moving local reptiles, but Sherry once
did. It was neither an anole nor a collared, but one of
the more prevalent northern prairie lizards. She had
been watching it at close range for some time before
she finally decided to risk the attempt. Slowly she
reached out a finger and gently stroked the little creature's spine while he closed his eyes in contentment
and made an almost inaudible purring sound that reminded her, she said, of a tiny cat. I can see why some
people make pets of lizards and their kind.

Back in Cook County, my brother, Tom, kept a pet
iguana. He used to astound the neighborhood when
he would put on its little collar and leash and take it
for walks around the block. It grew to a full twenty-
seven inches before it finally died late one evening. As
Tom had to go to school the next day and wanted to
give his departed a proper daylight burial, he wrapped
it in newspaper and put it in the freezer. Procrastination set in. Weeks turned to months. All but forgotten, the deceased was shuffled to the back of the
freezer.

I wish I had been there the day my elderly aunt (the high-strung one with the hair-trigger nerves), knowing nothing of the frozen twenty-seven-inch lizard, was sorting through the freezer's contents looking for something with which to make supper . . . ah well. These things happen.

While pools of sunlight spread slowly outward from the butternut, the chinkapin, and a nearby red-bud tree, most of this area remains shaded. The rocky glade above the spring has fewer eastern trees to block the sun. With the thought that it will be warmer there, I begin to make my way in its general direction. Sherry mentioned that while jogging yesterday she saw a water moccasin in the largest of its two ponds. I'd like to get a look at it. Snakes often live a decade or more, so there's a chance it may be the same snake with whom I had an encounter some years back.

A friend of mine had lent me her silver flute, and another friend was providing me with informal lessons. Dressed in cutoff jeans, the two of us, each with flute in hand, were wading in the pond I have dubbed the Western Sea. I had gotten into an easy flow with the borrowed flute and was in the midst of parleying back and forth with several birds who had drawn near to listen, when not more than eighteen inches from where I stood in the shallow water my eyes came to rest upon the water moccasin.

Upon spotting me, it shot upward from its sub-merged coils until its beady eyes glared at me from well above the surface of the water. Its open jaws and the full diamond spread of its head made it clear that it would strike at the slightest provocation.

Considering that water moccasins are the most dangerous and aggressive of all North American pit vipers, to this day I can offer no explanation for my instantaneous reaction. Continuing to play the flute, I swayed back and forth to the music just as I had been—my playing even seemed to improve under the pressure. I had been doing this only a few seconds, maintaining eye contact with the snake all the while, when my mind was suddenly filled with the remarkably clear image of an Indian snake charmer. Had I not been so afraid I would have laughed.

The most bizarre feature of what followed was the water moccasin's response. His head began swaying back and forth to the music, following my movements as closely as a cobra rising from a fakir's basket. And while he so proficiently played the part of the serenaded serpent, I found myself, with no conscious effort, playing a flute melody that moments before I would have thought beyond my ability.

Our respective movements became so thoroughly synchronized that for a while we both seemed to lose ourselves in the larger event. My concern, however, had not entirely vanished, for I realized later that even while I had been fully attentive to my playing, my body had been slowly edging away toward the safety of the rocky shore. The encounter ended peacefully, with a somewhat disappointed snake swimming off in search of more dedicated, or perhaps tastier, entertainment.

As I prepare to leave the First Rocks to revisit the site of this incident, I find that its memory has heightened my awareness of my surroundings. At first I think it strange that so detailed a recollection of a past event could bring me a heightened perception of the present. Yet I've often noticed that powerful experiences of being wholly attentive to the present moment have a curious link with one another that can sometimes make events a decade apart seem separated by no more than a few moments.

Perhaps this is the real magic of the present. When one is truly experiencing the now, one is simultaneously aware of all other nows, as if in some incomprehensible way past and future are merely the projections of creatures who imagine their own beginnings and endings in terms far more absolute than any recognized by nature.

Entire epochs are compressed in this solitary now. The past is here. Encoded in these rocks, in these trees, in the multitudes of tiny lives that daily work this soil. Without the past there would be no soil, and without soil there would be no life.

WALKING SLOWLY, MY BARE FEET enjoying the feel
of the moist earth beneath them, I pause for a moment to notice a footprint I have left in the soft
ground. It brings to mind one of the strangest things
I have ever seen. In a thickly wooded ravine, many
miles from any human habitation besides our own,
four of us saw it—the impossible—right there before
us in the damp morning soil. Small. Child-sized.
Made, it seemed, but moments before. It was a single
human footprint.

We stared.

There were no other prints around. And no way—
within the framework of all we knew—that lone print
could be explained. Silently we each arrived at the
same conclusion: This was something we would keep
to ourselves. We had no wish to jeopardize the wild,
hidden life of whoever, or whatever, had made that
tiny naked print. It has been nearly twenty years
since that morning. This area is much more settled
now. It may be that I will never see another, yet that
flicker of hope remains, and even as I turn my attention to other things, it leaves me with the thought,
Today may be the day.

The sun is now well above the horizon, yet overhead is such an intertwining of leaf-covered branches
that much of the path remains shaded. The air above

it is cool and damp, and its dampness accentuates the smells of spring.

Over a thousand species of trees, wildflowers, vines, shrubs, herbs, and berries are native to this area—and more than *two thousand* species of mosses, lichens, liverworts, and fungi. Which of them now blend their scents to bring me so rich and satisfying a fragrance I can't say, but this forest's aromatic ambiance is one of its qualities I most love. Its emphasis changes with the seasons, yet consistently through them all—even in the midst of winter—there is something in the air here that is so earthy, so sensuous, so pervasive and alchemically alive, for me it has become the scent of home.

Here, to the south of the path, a small ravine slopes down to contribute its runoff to the creek's periodic flow. Over the centuries its last hundred yards have eroded into a gently sloping basin where a grove of oaks shares the company of a hickory and a mammoth old pine.

These are big trees for this region, all of them over a century old. The sun is still low enough to emphasize the bold lines of their trunks, which stand out more prominently now than they will later in the day. In the rich soil of Iowa or Virginia, trees of their age would be much larger, but in this rocky Ozark soil, they have done well to survive at all.

The oldest and largest tree on our land, but for one, is a classic white oak in front of the farmhouse. A local forest ranger once estimated its age between 250 and 300 years. We call it the Conference Oak because for years it served as the gathering place for those who met to help us prevent a large tract of adjacent forest from being clear-cut. In the end our efforts were successful, yet without that old oak they might have never begun.

We were just ending the seven years of isolation that Sherry and I refer to as our "media fast," and I had never before spoken publicly. Some thirty to forty neighbors had gathered along with the editor of our local paper to hear me outline our plan for saving the forest. I was so intimidated by the prospect of talking to that many people, I had nearly decided to back out of speaking. When I confided this to a friend whose work involved lecturing, he took me aside and pointed out that if I did not share the details of my initiative, most of the trees between our home and the river would be destroyed.

His reminder brought me to my senses. Although we did not own the threatened land, we often hiked and picnicked there, and we had grown to love its trees. When I thought of them leveled, personal comfort became secondary. My proposal had to be shared, fear or not. By focusing on my love for the trees, rather than on my fear, I was able to make a start. Sitting with my back to the Conference Oak as I spoke, I felt a powerful calming influence coming from the tree. It filled me with a quiet strength that helped me find the confidence I needed.

These trees here along the spring path are not so old as the Conference Oak, but even at this distance I feel from them the same gentle power—and for them, the same love. How much trees give to us! Besides the obvious value of their wood, they contribute to our lives in ways we often overlook. Not least of these is the gentle strength that radiates from older, mature trees and seems to have a subtle calming effect on all within range.

Though I have tried to be silent in my approach, I startle a doe, who leaps off—one, two, three zigzag bounds—then pauses, turning to look curiously back at me. To my right and left, squirrels, too, dart off noisily through the leaves, unsure of what a creature like me might have for breakfast, and taking no chances.

With care I skirt the edge of a carpet of tiny bluet flowers and enter the open rocky area above the spring. I move quietly. If I come upon the snake Sherry saw yesterday, I don't want it slithering off into the water before I have a chance to look at it. Not that snakes are particularly timid. Of all the forest creatures they seem the least bothered by a human presence. But examining the shores of the pool where the encounter occurred, as well as the smaller pool in the area's midlands, I see no sign of any snake, water moccasin or otherwise. At this time of day I would think a reptile would be warming itself somewhere in the sun, but I see only the usual assortment of northern prairie lizards.

Climbing down alongside the waterfall that trickles into the spring basin, I enter an area of such majestic diversity it defies simple description. The basin—now entirely in the sunlight—is about seventy-five feet in diameter. It lies like a sunken horseshoe in the middle of the creek, its open end facing toward the east. The cave from which the spring flows stretches along the basin's western rim, its ceiling, the same ledge of bedrock that forms the floor of the open area above. Here it extends outward a full fifteen feet—a twenty-foot slab of stone, two feet thick, which appears to hang suspended in space with no visible sign of support.

The first time I saw it I was reminded of the cantilevered concrete ceilings in Frank Lloyd Wright's Falling Water House, which as a child I once toured with my father. Built above a creek much like this one, the house is noted for a series of impossibly massive concrete weights that appear to float unsupported in the air or to rest on walls of open glass. Here, of course, there is no pretense of supporting glass, but the effect is equally impressive.

The south of the basin features the columns that support the ledge after it curves eastward and finally makes a reluctant concession to gravity. On first glance these columns appear to be composed of clay, soft and malleable, but hands-on inspection shows that they are rock—and as solid as any Parthenon. From top to bottom they are riddled with openings that resemble the mouths of tiny caves, and their unusually shaped surface features are covered with strange and curious etchings.

Beneath the northwestern corner of the ledge grows an extravagant tangle of intermingled grape and poison ivy vines. This is a hazardous combination, for the thought of succulent mouthfuls of wild grapes is not easily put out of mind; and each October this patch draws adults and children alike into a botanical version of tag—with scrumptious prizes for those who avoid contact, and a burning rash for those whom the ivy tags.

The wild grape is smaller and less sweet than commercially grown varieties, but it has a flavor I wouldn't trade for Napa Valley's finest. In this damp soil the vines never fail to produce bumper crops of the tart, purple fruit. Despite the ivy, this is our favorite place to gather them, for it involves no climbing.

Most of the grapes we gather for pressing into juice come from high in the trees, where the vine's parasitic nature always presents me with something of a dilemma. The diameter of a mature grape vine will often exceed the thickness of an adult's leg as it spirals into the highest branches of a tree, competing with its leaves for light until the tree eventually dies. Often I find myself facing the choice of whether to leave the vines or to cut them back in order to save the tree.

In this forest, which after the logging of the last century is only now beginning to regain something of its former maturity, my rule of thumb is to leave the grape vines on trees less than a hundred years old and to cut them back only on the older trees.

The children are happy either way. While they love the grapes and will often climb forty or fifty feet into the uppermost branches of a tree to claim but a few mouthfuls, they waste no time in exploring the swinging possibilities of the severed vines. Like cedar, grape vines resist decay and often last long enough to create minor erosion problems where years of children's takeoffs and landings have marked the soil with happy furrows.

It seemed unlikely earlier, but with the sun nearing its zenith the day has actually grown hot. My clothes suddenly feel stifling. Removing my shirt, the sun feels so warm and soothing on my skin that I am inspired to continue. Why not a bath? I think, shedding the rest of my clothes to wade in the cool, shallow water.

Twenty yards further down creek, the water is waist deep. Many blistering summer days, while waiting for the spring's slow trickle to fill my water jug, I have submerged myself there, head alone above the surface. While the air today is warm, the water remains icy from our still-near-freezing spring nights. A quick plunge would do me good. If I get too cold I can always come back to stretch out on these sunlit rocks.

The creek's slowly flowing water leads me easily through the impenetrable growth along its shores. New-budding branches massage my skin as I pass, waking me up, white body that I am, after my winter of indoor living.

From nature's point of view I expect our human winters are more like hibernation than actual living. Can any mammal truly *live* indoors? Admittedly, I find winter a stimulating season for the intellect. But for life? For its exhilaration and passion? Hardly. My spirit craves the outdoors, and at the moment, I suspect—with some residual left-brain trepidation—it wants a blast of that icy water. Without further thought I dive in, leaping to my feet in the same motion, panting furiously with involuntary, primitive passion. I'm alive now! No illusions. I'm freezing. Quick—to the warm rocks!

My body is shaking uncontrollably as I sprint awkwardly back into the sunlight, yet in some inexplicable way I feel more in control than ever, as though I have consciously induced and accepted these tremors in hopes they might shake loose the sluggish habits that have crystallized about me during the winter months. But the shaking quickly subsides as I stretch out on the sunlit rocks.

Resting my elbows on a patch of moss, head propped on my hands, I look into the clear, mirror-still waters of one of the many shallow pools that spread across the basin's floor. Playing with the inverted images of clouds and trees, I lapse into one of my favorite childhood games, imagining the reflection is the reality and the reality the reflection, seeing if I can convince my street-wise, wood-wise eyes that this is true—and noting the startling differences in perception when for fleeting seconds I succeed.

By the time I am dry, I am already feeling warm again. No need at present for jeans and heavy flannel shirt. From my backpack I withdraw my favorite pair of cutoffs, tossed in this morning as an afterthought. I hardly expected today's temperatures to grow warm enough for them, but I am grateful for the foresight that now allows me to proceed lightly clad.

How much experience we miss through these buffers we place between ourselves and the world. Oh, I don't suppose that clothing, when all is said and done, is the most significant of them; it may well be the least. But when you add together all our various and sundry insulating barriers (walls, floors, automobiles, streets, sidewalks, shoes that keep our feet from ever touching the earth, urban landscapes designed entirely around commercial priorities), when you add them all up and derive your sum, it is no wonder that we have come to regard ecology as a science rather than a way of life.

Yet the sum total of all these physical buffers insulates us not half as much, not one-tenth as much, no, not even one-hundredth as much as our languages and beliefs, for these have the disturbing tendency to lock us into concepts of ourselves and our world that deny all experience not snugly fitting their shallow definitions. They would probably smother us in our own conceptual carbon dioxide were it not for the activities we enjoy outdoors in the open air.

The wind raises tiny hairs on my arms and stomach. My skin comes alive, bringing me sensory information I rarely notice when clothed. When in the forest, I am always aware of sights, sounds, and smells, but it is rare that my sense of touch enters this fully into the picture. Yet *touch* may be too limiting a term for the subtle information gathered by exposed

skin. Except for the soles of my feet, I am not techni-
cally "touching" anything, yet through my skin my
body is far more aware of my environment than when
clothed.

I *hear* not a sound, but I suddenly *feel* something
enormous rolling through the world, shifting from the
west into the east. A change in atmospheric pressure.

The forest grows still, expectant.

In the near perfect silence I hear, far off in the distance, a deep and barely discernible rumble. Then
something enormous grabs hold of the rug beneath
the world and yanks back, sending ripples through
the fabric of my surroundings.

Trees on a distant hilltop bend low, shaking their
leaves in what appears a frenzy of joyous excitement.
But the breeze has not yet reached here, and while I
remain immersed in a silent, expectant stillness, I
watch the wind bow low the tops of trees nearer and
nearer until at last the gust hits me, carrying the
fresh scent of ozone and a hint of the distant sea.

Above, a hawk repeats some urgent cry, and for a
moment I mistake its call for a gull's. Yes, there is
rain behind this wind. No doubt now—there is thunder in the air. We may have a storm after all.

Time to reexamine these clouds. This is something
more than just a midday reconvening of the breakfast convention. In the west the lower clouds pass so
near to the ground that one momentarily obscures
the treetops on a distant ridge. Urgently they move
northward, as if late for some vital engagement on
the outskirts of Winnipeg or Saskatoon. High above
them are other, finer clouds hurrying in the opposite
direction.

Normally these high- and low-pressure areas feign
civility and attempt—if somewhat begrudgingly—at
due process, working out their differences peaceably

without resort to thunderous confrontation. But when negotiations fail, as it appears they now have, their disagreements spill over into the skies above our fields and streams, and we below are caught in the throes of battle. At the moment, northern forces seem to be challenging the south's air superiority—and the south is not taking it lying down. Events in these placid woods could soon take an exciting turn.

Because the Ozarks are the only mountain range in North America to run east to west, and because they are situated at the exact midpoint between the Arctic and the equator, for a good part of each year they become a seasonal battleground between the climates of north and south. Temperature fluctuations here can be truly extreme. I have seen the Fahrenheit thermometer read twenty degrees below zero and seventy degrees above during the same week.

The Ozarks are well suited to those who enjoy the coming of spring. Spring arrives here nine, ten, sometimes a dozen or more times each year. Our winters are so erratic that we may have a foot of snow as early as Thanksgiving or a December balmy enough to permit a swim in the river.

I'll not soon forget the December 22 I flew to Boston for two days. After weeks of sixty-degree temperatures, I packed only a sweater and a light coat—alas, no long underwear, boots, gloves; no ice scraper. Flying back into St. Louis a mere forty-eight hours later, ice and a foot of snow had covered everything. When I stepped off the plane, the thermometer read five degrees below zero. When I got my truck started two hours later, it read ten below. And by the time I slid sideways into an all-night gas station, hoping to purchase an ice scraper—an item completely sold out across the city—the mercury read fifteen degrees below zero. Wind chill, minus forty.

I should have known.

Like the Civil War, our weather pits north against south all winter long. Sometimes the north wins a battle, and cold Canadian air masses occupy our territory for a few days. Then the south comes back with an invading force of warm air from the Gulf of Mexico. All hell breaks loose as thunder cannons, and lightning splits the sky. If the southern forces carry the day, we may then have a period of balmy weather before the north returns—often with a vengeance—to battle again in another attempt to force the mercury downward.

But while this present hullabaloo may portend a storm, or even a tornado, it nevertheless remains my favorite form of entertainment. No Hollywood production has yet furnished me with enjoyment so deep and wholesome as a good old rip-roaring thunderstorm. "Yes!" a rumble answers from the west. Let the lightning flash, the thunder roar, crack, crash, and rumble; let the trees turn their leaves upside down and bow before the warring winds; let the sky open and the rains pour.

Beethoven at his stormiest could not entertain so well.

THE WIND HAS PICKED UP considerably now, and
the air carries the crisp, distinct smell of rain. From
my vantage point here above the spring I can make
out only a small portion of the dark clouds massing
beyond the northwestern ridge. A threatening, billowing, and altogether glorious incoming wave of
cloud is rolling slowly nearer. Some amazing things
are occurring in that sky, but from down here in the
creek bed I can see only a sliver of it.

A hundred feet up the hill is an oak that affords a
magnificent view. As I recall, it is a long way from the
forest floor to its first branch; but if I could somehow
make my way up there, it is good climbing after that
and an easy matter to attain its heights. With storm
clouds mounting overhead in Spielberg-style confu-
sion, the thought of a 360 degree view of open sky is
too much to resist.

There is not a moment to lose.

Quickly I gather my notebook and scattered
clothes, stuff them into my backpack, and shove it up
under the ledge, where it will remain dry. It may be
somewhat of a gamble, trusting to my southern sym-
pathies and leaving warmer attire behind, but life favors not its fence sitters. For better or for worse, I cast
my lot with the south and, attired in only my cutoffs,
waste no time in mounting the hill and making my

way to the base of this oldest and largest tree on our land.

Looking upward, however, I realize that the first branch is higher off the ground than I had thought. Fine time to remember. I measured it once. Twenty-eight feet. I had been hauling firewood from the area, and after noticing the tree's climbing possibilities, I returned for the next load with an aluminum extension ladder. When I reached that branch, before climbing further upward, I dropped my twenty-five-foot tape measure only to watch it extend to its full length and swing back and forth, still a good three feet above the ground. That was the only time I'd climbed the tree, and only the ladder had enabled me to reach that branch. Now what? Its trunk is too large to shinny up. My arms reach barely halfway around its eight-foot girth.

Ladderless, I study its massive trunk as it looms upward toward that enticing limb, wondering if there is some other way to achieve it. A pine sapling grows nearby. Examining it, an idea forms—and it just might work. If I were to climb it to a height six or seven feet above that branch, then lean over until my weight bent the sapling near enough, I could probably climb on over into the oak. From there the rest would be easy.

Knowing that too much thinking about this will only provoke doubt, I climb the little sapling to the desired height. Next I must throw my weight in the direction of the oak. The tree is green enough that I have no fear of it snapping, but I have to get it right the first time. Once the sapling has bent under my weight, there will be no way to change its direction without climbing down and starting over—a repetition my naked thighs would likely veto.

A rumble of thunder in the northwest, closer than before, reminds me that I haven't much time. It's now or never. I throw my weight. The tree bends— thankfully in the desired direction. As the oak's branch brushes my leg, I slide over upon it, the sapling springs back, and in less time than it takes to describe, I am seated in the ancient tree's lowest branch, holding one of its vertical shoots.

With the storm fast approaching and my ultimate goal so near, I scoot quickly down to the trunk and begin my climb. Fortune favors those who act boldly, and I want that view!

Through the oak's prolifically branched interior I make my way upward until the last fading remnant of its once-mighty trunk divides into a final V-shaped pair of branches, each about the diameter of an ankle.

What an awesome sweep of sky! I had forgotten how expansive things looked from up here. Carefully I inch my way higher, one foot wedged in the crotch of that final V, a leg wrapped around its largest up- right. My arms embrace branches whose diameters are no greater than their own, my hands tightening fingers around branches smaller still.

My view is panoramic, sweeping, magnificent, and I am instantly rewarded with a flash of lightning. A pause—four, five, six—the seventh second brings a sat- isfying climax of thunder, accompanied by a gust of wind. The treetop sways wildly. My added weight car- ries it further than it would lean without me—a good five feet from its vertical position. As the return sway is met with another gust that blows us back again, for a moment I seem to float suspended between earth and sky . . . and it occurs to me that my assessment of this branch's weight-bearing capacity has hinged solely on my experiences of windless afternoons. But

the moment of uncertainty passes. A fierce joy explodes within me, and for no logical reason, I get the
distinct impression that this tree is aware of my presence and will protect me somehow so long as I am here.

Conventional wisdom holds that one should never
seek shelter beneath a tree in a thunderstorm, let
alone climb to the top of the tallest tree on a ridge
and immerse oneself in the very struggle of the elements. But as Mark Twain once observed, "A man
who is destined to be hung need not fear drowning."
And somehow I know with a certainty I count as in-
fallible that I am not to die so glorious and straight-
forward a death as to be struck by lightning—not
while in the top of this or any tree. I do not pretend
to know how I will go, but I'll give any takers seven
to three that it will not be by lightning.

A jagged fork winks agreement from the west.

Its image is still fading from my retina as its thunder sounds. Three seconds this time between lightning and thunder. Does that mean the storm is three
miles away? It seemed closer, but then the lightning
may not have come from the nearest portion of the
tempest, which madly tosses the trees on the far side
of the pasture. That would make it less than a quarter mile away. Well, quickly come, quickly gone, as
they say. A storm that blows in this rapidly will not
usually last long—a fact, I begin to suspect, of which
I may soon be glad.

Another, and brighter, electrical discharge races
through the western sky, instantly bringing to mind
the words of historian Bill Thompson, "Lightning has
struck the darkness we call reality. We pause now in
that brief interval between the lightning and the
thunder."

Even as the word *thunder* crosses my thoughts, its
reality seems to split the very ground in which this

tree is rooted. It sounds as though the rocks themselves were shattering, disgorging some incalculable
subterranean power.

How can nothing more than air sound so much like
boulders shattering? Like mountains being ripped
asunder? "Because air is as tangible as you are!" the
wind answers with a cold blast that shakes the tree
and brings me a fleeting image of some monstrous
hand trying to drop this human apple to the ground.

Fine time for my doubts to return, but they take
advantage of this grim thought and rush in with a
vengeance. The first drops of a cold rain begin to fall.
Maybe I was a little hasty, brushing my doubts off so
rudely when they sought to plead their case back on
the forest floor. But they take advantage of that
thought, too, and bitterly assault me with a chorus
of I-told-you-so's. Apparently this arboreal roller
coaster hurdles through emotional as well as physical
dimensions. I may as well accept it. There ain't no
gettin' off this ride till it's over.

It's not that I'll have difficulty holding on. Even
soaking wet the texture and placement of these
branches and the coarseness of their bark make keeping my grip a relatively easy matter. My concern now
is cold, for an icy rain has begun to pelt my skin. I
make a deliberate effort to relax. It takes all the
willpower I can muster, but at last I succeed. My
body continues to tremble, while within I remain,
well, almost calm.

The shaking of my arms suggests that my flesh
must have some mind of its own. Intent on warmth
through every possible means, my body bypasses usual
neocortex decision making and goes for it by the
quickest route: shivers! A heat-producing mechanism,
and a natural form of exercise, though rarely, I suspect, does it accelerate to this level of chaotic intensity,

a level so active at the moment that my shivering may actually be aerobic. *Aerobic Shivering?* I cough out an involuntary laugh. But I laugh too much, too long, almost hysterically; and this worries me a bit. A more sober part of me considers it in bad taste, but the laughter, I notice, also produces body heat.

The rain falls harder. My view is reduced to a blurry, blue-gray mist as the battling air masses rain what must be bucketfuls on each square yard of thirsty ground.

Yet even in the midst of this I would have to be uncommonly dull not to feel the sense of celebration that pervades these trees. They are ecstatic. It has been months since we've had such a good rain, and a long time indeed since they've been deluged by a spring shower like this one.

As if trying to compensate for depriving me of my view, the storm converts my treetop into a wild, dizzying ride that I'm sure would be outlawed at any responsible amusement park. No longer just five, but eight or more feet, this Ken-encumbered treetop is tossed to and fro, at times snapping back so quickly all thought of cold is banished in a flush of excitement that must rival what the wealthy seek through skydiving, parachuting, and other costly sports.

Many would regard my voluntary presence up here as indication of insanity—perhaps even feel rather certain of it. But something my grandmother once said comes back to me now in the midst of this dizzying storm. Great-grandma O'Leary's daughter. I can almost see her kindly face drift up before me in the blur of wild rain.

"Larry," she said to me—for you see, time had stopped for granny one day back in the 1930s and she thought I was her grown son, Larry, when he was a boy—"Larry," she said in her thick old-country brogue, "'tis a gift God gives to those 'uns he chooses. In some, the peoples roundabout calls it genius, in others, crazy. But 'tis a gift, Larry, and 'tis up to you what you make of it. Make of it what you will, for one way or t'other—" and here she winked conspiratori- ally, "when the long road is over, you won't look back and see you haven't lived."

In a nation where it is respectable, even admirable, for corporate executives to pay hundreds of dollars to be shoved out of hot air balloons with 150-foot rubber bands tied round their waists, I think I could make a satisfactory case for the logic of climbing a tree. Even on such a stormy day as this. And with my grand- mother's wisdom—we Carey kids learned to make do with what we had—I will both introduce and rest my case, for if there is one thing I know for certain, there's no way in hell I'm ever going to look back on this life and see I haven't lived. Although it is possible I may one day look back and see how I could have lived longer.

Up here in the wind and the cold, I get the same feeling I used to get treading the fifty-nine-degree waters off the beaches of Santa Cruz, waiting to catch that next homeward wave, the same sense I got standing on that board, riding it into shore, balancing on the living surface of a planet more ocean than land. Besides the cold itself, which even a wet suit could not keep fully at bay, what I most remember about treading those heaving Pacific waters is a sense of the elements—and the energy that infuses them— almost identical to what I'm experiencing now.

Water pours so voluminously (or is the word volup- tuously?) over my face, I have only to hold out my lower lip to catch enough for a drink. I feel baptized by this wind and rain. Full immersion. In a watery sky. As this moment holds me attentively enthralled, a purification is taking place within me—I can feel it—a making new, a rebirth. But it's C-O-L-D! Bone-chilling cold.

The petty concerns that troubled me yesterday at this hour seem so ungodly frivolous and unimportant now; it is a struggle even to remember what they were. Although, when I stop to think of it, I do feel a sort of fondness for my past: my warm lamplit room, a fire crackling in the stove, books lining the walls, one of them propped open beside the salt and pepper shakers. And perhaps a bowl of chowder—ah, yes, New England clam chowder—steaming on the table before me.

But I must snap out of this. I've heard of people falling asleep in snow drifts, and for all its seeming improbability, for a moment just then I felt the draw of a similar spell.

The storm must be at its height. Wind-driven rain is falling with such furor, whipping this tree so rapidly about, that my vision sees surroundings gone all obscure and gray—a blurry mist of thrashing leaves, punctuated by flashes of lightning so intense each freezes a picture in my mind, an image that lingers with more reality than the darkness that instantly closes in behind.

And it *is* dark; too dark for midday.

My certainty wavers. The joy that only what, seconds? minutes? ago sent my fears scattering is now gone, and in the ambivalent vacuum of its wake, my fears return, stealthily—like rats who sense the coast is clear.

Thunder and lightning come simultaneously now, and with each blinding flash, bizarre snapshots imprint upon my mind, each one showing, revealing such a different world.

A new flash startles me with the turbulence it reveals. Are all storms perceived this way by foolhardy
humans in the tops of sixty-foot trees? Maybe it is
imagination, but I feel—got to be imagination—an
almost malevolent energy. *Just in relation to you,* my
spirit shoots back. *Nothing personal, Ken. Here in the
midst of their domain you're a rather negligible factor to
these thunder beings, to these energy titans clashing in
this tempest that in all likelihood is just an ordinary
storm—a storm like many accompanying the great temperature battles of spring.* Right, spirit, right. I want to
believe you, but—

Lightning flashes, thunder cracks, and in an instant the world I saw so recently in majestic spring-
time bloom appears dark, hideous. In the cold rain
that follows, my mind contracts, but the image remains. I see a forest identical to the one I know and
love, interpreted grotesquely somehow, as if in carica-
ture. The image is so compelling that my fear, whatever merit it may or may not possess, seems suddenly
of less relevance than the question of how this profound interpretive difference occurs.

*How you understand yourself determines what you
see; it determines your reality. There is a lesson here,
something to be learned from fear. If you think you can
be threatened, Ken, you are. Understanding, compre-
hending, you know that "you" could never be at risk,
though "who you think you are" could very well be, and
probably now is.*

Whatever.

I wish it would all go away. I never expected this
storm to become so intense. Yet as another ill-timed
flash shows me surrounded once more by that strange
and unfamiliar landscape, I feel more curiosity than
fear. Within me the familiar and the unfamiliar clash

as violently as these temperature battalions without. Could there be a connection?

Breathing deeply, I draw the charged air of the mingling fronts into my lungs. Evoking my love for this forest, this swaying, sodden branch to which I cling, the wave of panic falls away. In the lightning's next near-blinding revelation, my surroundings reappear in familiar tones—a bright, welcome reinstatement of the world I know. The sense of apartness dissolves, and I have to admit, I *am* enjoying all this. Not the fear, no, and certainly not the cold; but the uniqueness of the experience, and the learning that accompanies it.

To live in fear of risk and wonder is to exchange *life* for a secure somnolence in which one dies by degrees. The inner gambler is important to me. To deny it would be to deny a vital part of myself. Still, climbing this high in a thunderstorm is probably not one of the brightest things I've ever done.

Over these past—how long now?—it can be no more than a few minutes, I have felt several times a returning of what I can only describe as a wave of fear. Thankfully it has receded each time, but what I find puzzling is that it always seems to rise from below then fall away downward, as if it springs from an ocean of some heavy substance ordinarily deep within the earth but now, storm-tossed and turbulent, thrust upward from its usual sphere.

However, of far more interest to me than the apparent directional properties of these fearful waves are the perceptual alterations that accompany them. Each one leaves me feeling as though I am poised on the brink of some impending revelation, about to understand something Huge. Significant. If I could just put a finger on it. Apparently I am encountering archetypes up here, polarities, the twin extremes of what in our daily lives we usually encounter by degrees, unaware of how profoundly love and fear affect our perception.

Ordinarily the perceptual shifts that accompany love and fear pass unnoticed. Little loves, little fears—and frequent mixtures of the two—bring less discernible alterations. But in this war of elements, I am amazed at how dramatically the world appears to change when my heart is gripped, even for a few seconds, with so unfamiliar a depth of fear.

The image of my surroundings I see at such times reminds me of how they might look on a photographic negative. And even as the analogy comes to mind, another lightning explosion shows me bony, green-white branches stretched above a purple hillside alive with pale fluorescent boulders and other—!? It all came and went so quickly, I don't know if it is accurate to say other unidentifiable life forms. But that's exactly what they looked like.

What is that world? Why does it evoke such hauntingly familiar feelings? I am attracted to it and simultaneously repulsed. Intuition tells me that living, that is, *biological* creatures do not normally inhabit or even perceive it. Yet in that last flash I glimpsed some kind of creature or creatures unlike any I've ever seen. Could I hold that image for more than a single flash? The wind has abated somewhat, but while the rain continues to fall the exercise will give me something to take my mind off the cold. Besides, a chance to study this phenomenon may never come again. My decision is made. I'll try to sustain that view long enough to learn more of the world it reveals.

The interpretation has been so impressed upon me that as I close my eyes it is easy to visualize it once more. My mind brings the image into sharp focus; I hold it for a moment or two, then look up, eyes open. The eerie, strangely colored world remains, appearing quite real and carrying a distinct physical quality, although I am sure a camera would reveal nothing beyond the ordinary. What has changed is not the forest but my own way of visually interpreting it. This much is clear. What intrigues me is *why* this particular interpretation, and why it comes so easily.

Could my eyes have suddenly picked up an additional range of the spectrum? I have heard that the human eye is able to detect a broader range of the light spectrum than is usually admitted to consciousness. Perhaps in some long-ago forest what is revealed by the light of these other frequencies was regarded as peripheral—or even harmful—to the development of our species.

Yet, oddly enough, my body seems to regard this negative world as familiar and nonthreatening, as if my body may be aware of it on a regular basis, even while consciously I am not.

Have I stepped, like some Alice, through the looking glass?

This is clearly not the invisible world I saw as a child—the realm of metaform, archetype, and mathematical ideation. Nor is it the noosphere of Teilhard de Chardin, or some esoteric higher plane. It is the same visible world I see every day, interpreted inversely somehow—although, as I noted a moment ago, I did see in it some kind of creature or entity that I am certain has no biological counterpart.

Even as these thoughts occur, I begin to feel a growing sense of trespass, as though I am doing something wrong by holding this interpretation. Probing into it, I realize that for some time I have been subconsciously sensing that this world belongs to entities whose natures allow them to perceive it this way, creatures who lack the sensory emphasis of biological form. This is not to say that they lack forms necessarily, but like finer gaseous substances, they would probably be invisible by light of day.

I am reminded of Sting's *all the angels, all the devils, all around us, can't you see;* of C. S. Lewis's *eldila;* and of the graphic accounts in Frank Peretti's novels of unseen spirits influencing his characters for good or for ill.

It would be inaccurate to label this realm the world of the dead. Yet, if I am not mistaken, this is what humans have always called it. Hell to some, heaven to others, I dare say, it, too, could be interpreted in many different ways according to the loves and fears of those who have passed through the veil. In that respect, as all eventually discover, the mere shedding of biological clothing changes little. Emotional habits and spiritual predispositions endure for all, on both sides of the veil, until that significant moment when one chooses to open one's heart to love—and to love's eternal source.

My impression is that humans do sometimes walk through landscapes like the one I see below me, but they could hardly be ordinary people—sorcerers perhaps, saints, those in dire extremity, and maybe a few who meddle in things they do not understand. I may well be in that last category myself.

Breathing deeply, while once more closing my eyes, I release the fear and its strangely inverted interpretation. With its departure an unexpected surge of love floods through me, and I resolve in the future to leave this path to those who are called. Slowly I open my eyes upon a wet but familiar world.

The rain has stopped; the storm is all but ended.

For some minutes my mind knows only a silent stillness within, a meditation without effort, a celebration of occasion. Slowly my vision focuses on a bird of red-streaked chocolate-colored feathers and bright orange beak. She rests in a nearby tree, encircled by glistening leaves to which crystal-droplet remnants of the rain cling briefly before they fall. I have been watching her a long while now without registering, labeling, or defining her particular condensation of being, taking her as much for granted as she appears to take me. So beautiful. So natural. A bird in a tree.

As if by magic—higher in the sky than I would have guessed—the sun breaks through the clouds to shine upon the very bird who centers both my thoughts and field of vision. So unlikely an occurrence seems almost a miracle.

What wonders went before now pale as the sun breaks out in all its glory. On every leaf, water droplets sparkle and gleam like thousands of tiny suns to fall, one by one, then reappear as new moisture beads in their place, and gentle breezes ruffle the leaves to which they cling.

How long, I wonder, have I been up in this tree? It seems nigh on eternity, and I suppose it may well be, if eternity is defined by the depth of experience in moments taken wholly as they are.

Every fiber of my being tells me that I belong here as much as the female cardinal the sun lights across the way, as much as the wisps of cloud hurrying northward through the clearing skies above, as much as the ant crawling complacently across my still-dripping, rain-reddened foot, pausing halfway—as if the storm had never been—to lap water from a bead of moisture that rests, wild jewelry, upon my skin.

This ant has likely seen as many storms in this tree as the cardinal in the tenement across from me. I am honored that she accepts me enough to have that drink, to amble boldly afterward down my heel and continue industriously on her way.

I have been given an assurance here today that I will take back with me to my human world, a strength that aligns me with a world of friends and forces unseen, a stability of self that will help me maintain my balance amid the demands of life's ever-fluctuating concerns. In aboriginal fashion, through the wilderness of human affairs, it will guide me, I know, so long as I honor it.

BALANCE, NATURE'S CARDINAL RULE, asserts in this moment a check to my newfound assurance. How will I get down from this tree? In my hurry to view the storm from its heights, I had not stopped to consider that. It may be wise to climb down to that lowest branch and give it some thought.

As I shinny down a southern face of upper trunk, already warm from its short while in the sunlight, the spongy wooded texture of its rain-soaked bark feels so good against the skin of my stomach and thighs, and the unobstructed light of a sun an hour past its noon so warm and soothing upon my back, I pause longer than necessary if the forest floor were my only goal; but it is not. One way or another I am certain I will end up down there—we all do one day—so I see no need to deny myself a full experience of what I may happen to encounter on the way.

There is a Zen story of a monk who is chased by a tiger halfway up a cliff. While the tiger leaps up clawing at him from below, the monk looks up and notices two things: a ripe strawberry growing just inches from his face; and a second tiger, meaner and hungrier looking than the first, leaning over the top of the cliff awaiting him with an impatient growl. "So what does the monk do next?" wisdom asks rhetorically. *Eats the strawberry!* the enlightened reply.

Even now, faced with the challenge of how to reach the ground, warm sun and wet bark bring sensations too luxurious to hurry through. When at last I reach the tree's lowest branch—itself the size of many nearby trees—I straddle it, lean comfortably back into the massive trunk, and scan the ground below.

So near ... and yet so far. I've roofed enough buildings to know my limits. An eight-foot jump I can handle. Ten I can manage. If unavoidable, a twelve-foot jump is within my range, but barely. Leaps from any greater heights I attempt only when my body, snug in its bed, is conveniently left behind; and in this case, astral projection would solve only half the problem.

My house is less than a half mile away. If I were to call out for someone to fetch a ladder, they would probably— Well, actually, now that I think about it, they would never let me hear the end of it. I can imagine the grins on my children's faces if they had to *get Daddy*   *from a* *tree eee!*
                                 down

No! Tell me it isn't happening—the last thing I need right now—a crow! Flying overhead, calling out to his cronies. Oh, mother of nature, she is sparing no pains to ensure the preservation of *my* humility. Where was she when Whitman needed her! If there is anything calculated to bring out the worst in man or beast, it is the harassment of a crow; and God help anyone who ever gets on the wrong side of a whole flock.

I remember the infectious assault of an owl by first one, then three, then a dozen crows, black as a small thundercloud. Once I even saw a bald eagle overwhelmed by their raucous attacks—not a comforting thought as I hear my antagonist answered by a chorus from the far side of the pasture. Well, well. Could be worse. At least pterodactyls or monk-hungry tigers are not likely to show up.

The crow has stopped flying for the moment. From the periphery of my vision I see him perched menacingly in the tree across from me. I risk a quick glance. Tauntingly the chicken-sized bird looks me in the eye and opens his defiant beak. The decibel level of his call for reinforcements soars. I can just hear him saying, *Hell's bells, boys! Come and look at this will you? A half-naked human mammal thing trapped in the crotch of a tree. Caw, haw, haw!*

My only hope is to ignore him. If he succeeds in gathering his unruly flock, things could get ugly.

Events follow in the footsteps of our thoughts. I had best channel my thinking along more positive lines. Animals are adept at sensing the tone, if not the literal content, of our human thoughts. And while signs of agitation will only egg a crow on, a peaceful heart disgusts him and will usually send him hurrying on his way. Often I have noticed how readily animals, and especially birds, respond to such things as flattery. There's an idea! It would be a formidable task for an admitted crow bigot like me, but if somehow I could bring myself to think positively of the crow species . . .

Since nothing to recommend a crow comes to mind, I accept what does: a warm memory of one of the crow's nearest relatives, a raven, a particular raven, whose timely arrival once derailed my consideration of certain, shall I say, untimely themes.

The day I met the raven dawned through a gray mass of low-lying cloud that soon gave way to a slow drizzle. My family and I were driving across northern Scotland on our way to Iona, an island off its northwest coast long considered sacred by the peoples of northern Europe. For centuries pilgrims from around the world have journeyed to a monastery built there by Saint Columba in the eighth century. It had been chosen as the setting for a three-day seminar I had agreed to offer on the application of spiritual principles in daily life. I had written a book on the subject and was supposed to know something about it. Trouble was, sometimes I did, and sometimes I didn't.

I was told that people would be coming from all over Europe to attend the event, and I just wasn't feeling up to it. The evening before I had given a talk at the Findhorn Community; it was received well enough, but I knew that I had not really spoken from my heart. My talk had been more a product of memory than of passion, and my conscience was milking the fact for all it was worth.

At the port town of Oban, we drove our van onto a ferry that carried us to the island of Mull, which we would have to drive across to reach the fishing village where yet another ferry would take us to the island of Iona. *What have I gotten into?* I thought as we splashed along Mull's solitary one-lane road. Even the lush scenery and the kids' animated conversation about some rock group rumored to have a house somewhere on the island failed to cheer me. With every passing, rainy, drizzly mile, my spirits continued to nose-dive.

Vehicles are not permitted on Iona, so when we reached the tiny fishing village on the west coast of Mull, we parked the van and began loading our trunks and suitcases onto the other and much smaller ferry. As we heaped our luggage in a pile on the open deck, I was more depressed than I had ever been in my life.

My book had become a best-seller in its field and was at that time particularly popular in Britain. It spoke of approaching each moment with humor, love, and spontaneity, and extolled the virtues of positive thinking. The hundred or so people coming to this event would expect me to practice what I preached. I did, of course, *some* of the time, but I still had my bad days—and this whole week had been nothing but. All I wanted at the moment was to find the nearest pub, down a few pints, and, uh, adjust my attitude.

Our rain-drenched luggage piled on the slippery deck of the ferry seemed symbolic—too damn much stuff! As the boat slid away from the dock and the first waves began to spray up onto her deck, I almost wished one of them would just wash everything overboard, me included, and let me surface, panting, invigorated, and full of life again.

We finally arrived. Our friend Eleanor had given us the use of her cottage, a well-kept white-and-green affair on the main street facing the beach, just a stone's throw from the rocky shore. After we had stacked our dripping luggage in the front hall, Sherry and the children prepared to embark for an inn down the road renowned for its seafood dinners. I had been looking forward to this meal for weeks, but at the moment food was the farthest thing from my mind.

Since we had the house to ourselves, I told the family to go ahead and enjoy their dinner without me; I needed some time to think about things—alone. Pouring a bottle of Guinness Stout into a battered gray mug I found in a cupboard, I walked upstairs to one of the bedrooms and pulled a chair up to the window.

Outside the rain was blowing in violent sheets across the rapidly darkening sky. Less than thirty yards away I could see whitecaps crashing on the huge rocks that fronted the beach. The foam had barely settled on my Guinness, and I was just taking my first sips of the dark Irish beer, when a jet-black raven landed on the windowsill, just inches in front of me. From the other side of the glass he looked up at me from one eye, head cocked to the side, as if to say, *Let me in. Open the window and let me in!* With that he began pecking insistently on the glass. Concerned that opening the window might scare him away, I hesitated for a second, then decided to risk it.

Carefully I stood and began lifting the sash. I had raised it barely two inches when that little son of a Scottish crow ducked his head under, squeezed in, and without hesitation walked immediately up my arm, not stopping until he had reached my shoulder, where he casually took up position and began preening his dripping feathers as if he had known me all my life.

In as near as I ever want to get to a state of shock, I turned slowly to the side to verify that this was not a dream, that there really and truly was a large, wet bird on my shoulder. From inches away my eyes confirmed it. There he sat all right, contentedly drying his feathers. Noticing my gaze, he gave me an affectionate nip on the ear, a sort of patronizing gesture that reminded me of an adult tousling the hair of a child who is loved but not taken very seriously.

It was strange. I seemed to know what the raven was thinking. At the same time, I doubted whether a bird could think at all and suspected I was anthropomorphizing on all cylinders. Unable to resolve this on such short notice, I decided to put my doubts on hold. I knew that I could always get back to them later.

Opinions become prisons at a time like this. When taken too seriously, skepticism admits through its bars of bias only those facts that support it and denies everything that does not, especially if it happens to be unfamiliar. And I was clearly on unfamiliar ground. I felt a genuine liking for the raven. Why not accept him as an equal, as I would another of my own species? With the thought came a surge of affection and a sense that it connected us somehow, bridging our differences and providing a basis for exchange.

If the Buddhists were right, and all lives ultimately sprang from the same source, perhaps thought could be transferred along that link of mutual affection much as a telephone message is transferred along a wire. Maybe that's what was happening. Why not just assume that it was, and see if I couldn't strike up a conversation? It was worth a shot. In the dialogue that followed, I spoke aloud and intuitively translated the impressions I received from the raven into language. The words were mine, of course, but I like to think their meaning may have been his—or close to it.

How great a role my imagination played in our conversation I'll never know, but portions of our exchange dealt with points of view so at odds with my usual way of looking at things that it's difficult to believe I just imagined them. Not that it matters. The conversation was profoundly healing for me, and that, in and of itself, made it worthwhile.

"Well," I said aloud, uncertain how to begin, "uh—now that you're here, raven, what do you know?" (It was an awkward opening, but at the time I could think of nothing better.)

"If it's all the same to you," the raven shot back, "I'd rather stand on your head." And without waiting for an answer, he hopped up onto my stocking cap, sinking his little claws through its fabric into my skull.

"I came to ask you something," he said. "What are you afraid of?"

"I'm not afraid of anything," I returned defensively. "I'm feeling depressed, but I'm not afraid."

"You're afraid," the raven contradicted in a tone of such unassailable authority that I immediately saw

the futility of further argument. "You fear something," he went on. "What is it?"

For a while I sat silent, looking into my heart to
see if there might be some truth to what he said.
Gradually a light began to dawn. He was right. I was
afraid—afraid of being inadequate, of not living up to
expectations, of finding myself at a loss for words
during the coming seminar. Sensing that the bird had
followed my thoughts as closely as if I had spoken
them aloud, my verbal response was just a gloomy
summary.

"I don't really have all that much to offer them," I
said, feeling immediately better for having made the
admission. The simple statement seemed to clear the
air. Identifying my concern in the unambiguous
terms demanded by the raven made me feel that I
was once more in charge of my life, no longer a victim
but a creator of circumstance.

Dealing with depression had been like grappling
with some looming, nebulous, ever-present intangi-
ble. I could never get my hands on it; it was too non-
specific to resolve. In my failure to identify it clearly,
I had given it power over me. I could not understand,
much less resolve, a feeling as vague and gloomy as
the day's weather. But fear? Uncomfortable as it was,
it was something I understood.

The clarification put me back on familiar ground.
The confidence that had eluded me while under the
cloud of depression quickly returned. My fears remained, of course, but as I saw them for what they
were, they no longer troubled or intimidated me. They
were nothing I couldn't easily shine through, as I had,
in fact, many times before. I didn't need any elaborate
analysis of my fears, tracing them back to instances of
childhood rejection and other God-only-knows-how-
worthless, blame-somebody (anybody!) rubbish. I just

needed to crank up the old love generator and focus on the things in life that I cared about, things that mattered, things that were all around me: my family, happy and excited to be here; Iona's unbelievably beautiful seascape, so rugged, wild, unchanged after all these centuries; my health; a warm, cozy cottage sheltering me from the storm; the raven himself.

With the lifting of my gloom I remembered the genuine affection I felt for the people who were coming to the seminar, a few of them old friends whom I looked forward to seeing again.

Then, too, there was that seafood carryout dinner that Sherry would inevitably bring back for me; and since she knew me so well, she'd likely bring another pint of stout to help me wash it down. Maybe she'd even join me for a while. Suddenly my prospects didn't look so bad.

The shadow that had been over me had barely lifted when I was struck by the ludicrous nature of so serious an exchange with a bird. I had to laugh. A snatch of an old song came drifting up from a radio downstairs. Kids must be home, I thought, reaching for what stout remained in my mug.

"Come on up here, you guys. You won't believe this."

Just before they entered the room, the raven hopped from my head onto my shoulder, as if he regarded that as the proper form for greeting company. After some good-natured ribbing from my kids and a few photographs, the family retired, and the raven and I settled down to make a night of it.

Sherry had not failed me. With the frothy head of a freshly poured Guinness settling in my mug, I broke out the boxed seafood combination platter containing fresh shrimp, buttered lobster tail, smoked salmon, stir-fried vegetables, a generous seafood salad, French bread, and plenty of whole wheat crackers. At the sight, my appetite returned with a vengeance, determined to make up for lost time. There wasn't much conversation while we ate—I bought off the raven with crackers, tidbits, and portions I was unable to finish. When all but a few shells had been disposed of, I leaned back contentedly in my chair and shared what was most on my mind.

"What is it like," I asked, "being a bird on an island in the North Atlantic? Don't you get cold in the winter? Where do you go when it snows? What about friends? Enemies, too, for that matter—do you have many predators?"

"Well," he said, warming to his topic, "it's like this, you see . . . " And it was a long while (figuratively speaking, of course) before I was able to get a word in edgewise.

During the next few hours, the raven and I caught up on the times as if we were old acquaintances who had not seen each other for far too long. Our exchange was punctuated by contented silences of the type that occur between the closest of friends—tranquil pauses when we each retreated into our own thoughts to ponder and reflect upon our respective lives. During one of these interludes I inadvertently picked up a stray thought. The raven was thinking to himself: *What one raven knows all ravens know, so it is that I have recognized this man, this raven friend.*

It was an interesting concept, but what brought me up short was the realization that the raven assumed this was also how I had recognized him! I was so startled I spoke aloud, questioning him on this peculiar philosophy.

"Oh, it's not philosophy," he replied stiffly, acting insulted. "Ravens have no time for philosophy. It's the Sky I'm thinking of—the Sky we fly in our minds.

I am one raven when I am in these feathers, but I am Raven when I fly."

"I don't quite follow you."

"I am in my thoughts just as I am in the world. In the world, I am sometimes airborne and sometimes resting on a chimney or a branch of a tree, and it is the same when I am in my thoughts. Sometimes I land in these feathers and attend to my personal needs, but in my mind I often fly. When I fly, my thoughts lift me above this one raven into the Sky, where I am simply Raven."

"You mean, like, you are then, how to say it, *all* ravens?"

"No, but I am what all ravens are, and I know what all ravens know—at least all that is worthwhile. Flying in my thoughts doesn't make me all ravens, it just makes me Raven."

It took a few minutes for this idea to sink in. Finally, choosing my words carefully, I asked, "So when you are flying in your thoughts, that is, when you are Raven, you are in touch with a sort of collective raven consciousness? Is that it?"

This time he paused, as he had done several times before when puzzled over something I had said. I felt his mind probing mine to get at the root of what I meant by the term "collective raven consciousness." And I knew he wouldn't proceed until he knew exactly what I meant.

To him ambiguity was error. He seemed to look upon thoughts and emotions as an accountant would look at a column of figures, as if each thought and feeling had a precise numerical value, and putting mind and heart in as perfect order as a balance sheet was a simple matter of accurate definitions and math. Only when he was satisfied that he understood me correctly did he reply in the affirmative.

"Right," he said. "Raven and what you mean by your term are close enough to pass for the same thing, although there are shades of difference. But you should not be ignorant of this; your species functions in the same way."

"It does?"

"Of course, you're kidding me aren't you?" he asked, pecking me on the ear a few times, which seemed to be the raven equivalent of an elbow in the ribs. "All species work like that," he said. "That's how you recognized me, isn't it? You remembered, didn't you?"

I *had* been having some amazingly vivid images come to mind ever since he had entered the room— images of cold stone halls, torchlit processions, faces looming and receding, but I had formulated none of this into anything very concrete, and certainly nothing that I would term a memory. I had taken this succession of images for no more than half-conscious daydreams of the sort I often have. Vivid, interesting, and enjoyable, they had been drifting in and out of my awareness all the while this prodigious bird had been roosting on my cap, but I had not thought them of much importance.

When he intimated that my musings may have been actual memories, memories that I was somehow picking up from my own species' collective reservoir of such things, I decided it was time to go to bed. Later the application of this insight would result in my book *Return of the Bird Tribes,* but at the time it was more than I cared to grapple with so late at night. It had been a long and exhausting day, and I was ready for sleep.

Knowing it only proper to see a guest to the door, I cracked open the window and with some reluctance held out my arm, gesturing for the raven to climb down and go back out.

He refused! He was not about to reenter that cold, stormy night.

Repeatedly I tried to coax him down, opening the window wide, even reaching my arm outside and gesturing plainly with a nod of the head the direction I suggested he take. But no. Despite the fact that my meaning could hardly have been clearer, he had resumed his post up there on my cap, and no protestations on my part would convince him to leave. I was honored, of course, but our visit had lasted several hours and it was now quite late. Wanting nothing more than a good night's rest, I shrugged, wrapped a quilt around my shoulders, walked over to the bed, and eased myself slowly onto the mattress.

As I made the transition from vertical to horizontal, the raven calmly walked from the top of my head to its side, taking up a new post just above my right ear. It all seemed matter of course to him, as if he had been familiar with such maneuvers all his life.

He was still perched on the side of my head as I drifted off to sleep. That night I dreamed as I have never dreamed before or since. No standard nocturnal voyage into the unconscious of us two-legged critters. No, I spent the night in Raven—and I dreamt of flying! Flying high above ocean waves, watching sunsets through the evergreens, and huddling in bell towers while storms passed.

When I awoke in the cold predawn glow, that tenacious bird was snoozing contentedly on my stocking cap. When I sat up, he calmly walked back to the top of my head and resumed his perch, hopping down onto my shoulder only as we left the house to walk thoughtfully together along the beach, where Sherry joined us with the camera, taking photos and listening as I told her of my night's adventures.

(Some years later, after an abridged version of this story appeared in a national magazine, complete with a color photo of the raven on my shoulder, I received letters from people who told of having similar experiences with these remarkable birds. One Native American wrote to say that while such raven exchanges were not as common as they used to be, they were nevertheless a regular occurrence among many of the tribes of the Pacific northwest.)

But even miracles must end. Knowing it had to be done, I placed a few cracker crumbs on the flat top of an old concrete post and coaxed the raven down for breakfast. While he stood there eating, I turned and slowly walked away. I felt some sorrow at leaving him, but I was not about to go through the rest of my life with a bird on my head. Besides, neither the inspirational nature of our exchange nor the healing it produced had been able to prevent my cap from acquiring a generous layer of bird droppings. My urge to rinse it in the sea had grown too strong to ignore.

I am back in Missouri now, far from Iona's rugged shore, but on my office wall hangs a poster-size photograph of the raven standing on my shoulder that morning, while behind us a brilliant sunrise colors the eastern sky. Whenever I find myself tempted by the demons of discouragement or despair, I look at that confident little bird in the photo. Or think of him as I do now, stranded up here in this ancient tree. He straightens me out. Every time.

Indeed, there is not a crow in sight.

WITH THE STORM PAST, the air has warmed. Above, a few scattered regiments of southern cumuli hurry northward to consolidate their gains, while below, the damp world glistens in the clear light of a new and brighter sun. The rain has rinsed the pollen from the air, which shines with the sparkling freshness of the First Day.

Twenty-eight feet above the forest floor, I lean back into the massive trunk of this seventeenth-century oak, with no idea of how to get down. Some subtle prodding from the background of my thought suggests that this should worry me. But after having moved with this tree through the wind and rain, tossing in its upper branches through the wilds of an inner storm as fierce as the outer one, the tree's serenity now seems almost my own.

Yet even as sunlight falls on the branch I straddle, and my body drinks it in—knowing it as the nectar of a star—there it is again, that whisper, hinting that I lack sufficient concern. But I shake off the thought, realizing how perfect this moment truly is.

Funny how "worry" is drilled into us. It is the very first lie children are taught to believe: *You should be worried; there is something to be worried about.* How young we are programmed! Even kindergartners can't help but notice how worried all the grownups look.

In first grade my friends and I conferred among ourselves and concluded that the more worried a person looked, the more important they must be. The evidence seemed to support our theory. Our principal always looked more worried than any of our teachers, and after one memorable visit from the superintendent of schools, we were so impressed, so awed at how positively desperate the man looked, we imitated him for days afterward.

At the moment, however, I see no cause for concern. Growing old and dying in the fork of this tree seems unlikely, and while I find unacceptable the options for reaching the ground that have so far occurred to me, I follow the path of least resistance, appreciating the sun's warmth and enjoying my elevated view of the forest, wreathed now in soft mist, rising wraithlike between its trees. My trust in this moment's perfection inclines me to trust the future as well.

True, I would prefer to be back on terra firma, but until a reasonable form of downward mobility presents itself, there is not much point in getting all worked up about it. Maybe if I knew how to roll like a paratrooper, I'd chance it. Even then, these cutoffs wouldn't offer much protection from the brush below; and were I to roll much, I would likely find myself tumbling down the steep slope of the entire hillside to land, I am afraid, rather abruptly atop the spring, thereby seeing it from a perspective I would rather forgo—at least by that route.

So while the sunlight of this early afternoon bathes my skin and drives the storm's chill from my bones, I lean back into this ancient tree, look upward through its yellow-green leaves, and watch the blue sky and white clouds above.

How glorious it must be to sail so high and free, to drift so silently through the heavens. How nice it would be to enjoy even a short reprieve from gravity, to have magical powers that would mitigate their forces somehow while I leapt and landed lightly in the leaves. *But you do have magical powers,* a thought suggests from some dubious corner of my psyche.

While I am instinctively wary of any reasoning that could possibly follow such a shaky premise, I must admit, this opening line has certainly piqued my interest. There is an outside chance this train of thought may lead to some truth, though I think it far more likely to begin and end in pride. Still, with time to pass, I may as well give it a few attentive rails to ride upon. I can always tear up the track if I don't like the direction in which it takes me.

No sooner have I decided this when my thoughts are whisked away into a memory, their direction clear and seemingly innocent.

A friend of mine, Tom Rowley, headed up the three-man crew that was building a new house in Mountain View for Dan Perry, a retired army sergeant with whom I had worked some years earlier. Tom had contracted the job, and George Momper and I had hired on. We had framed-in the house, shingled the roof to keep our work dry, and were then in the process of tackling the interior. It was a three-story structure, including a full concrete basement. At this early stage of its construction, the stairwell that would eventually join the three levels had not yet been completed. We had framed-in the stairwell openings on each floor, leaving a gaping four-by-eight-foot hole that ran the full three stories down through the center of the building.

At the time of this incident I was twelve feet above the plywood floor of the top story, installing insulation between rafters directly over the stairwell opening. Thirty feet below me was the solid concrete floor of the basement, littered at that moment with nail-studded scraps that we had been tossing down.

Outside I heard a vehicle pull into the yard and unload its passengers. Their voices soon identified them as George's wife, Marilyn, their children, Delany and Malachi, and—I was happy to hear—our son, Patrick. I had been telling Pat about the project and hoping for a chance to show him around. It would be good to see him and his friends. Days on the construction site were long, and even just a brief hello would be a welcome break from the tedium of stapling up insulation.

Until we built the stairs, we maintained a small access hole about ten feet to the west of the stairwell opening. The top of a ladder was visible there, and shortly after the children arrived I heard one of them climbing up it. From atop my own ladder above the stairwell, my line of vision allowed me to see the point where the child would soon emerge.

I smiled in happy greeting as I saw Delany poke her head up above floor level, climb quickly onto the plywood subfloor and look up at me with a bright-eyed welcome that made me feel as though I were one of her favorite people.

Smiling and walking toward me, she began describing something she had done that day, and before either of us knew what had happened she had stepped off the top floor into the opening that dropped three floors down into the basement.

The events of the next few seconds were extraordinary. Even years later I do not claim to understand them, but strange as it may sound, while they were actually occurring they seemed the most natural thing in the world.

When Delany stepped off into space, I was looking down at her from atop my ladder, feeling a warm

glow of welcome and affection. At that same moment, she was looking up at me. Seconds before she
took her fateful step, we had made eye contact—and
we did not break it now. While she seemed to pause,
suspended in midair above the opening, our eye contact continued.

Her expression toward me was one of complete
and total trust, as if on some level she knew, or believed, that I would not let her come to any harm. For
what reason I know not, but I felt no fear, no panic,
no reaction. Irrational as it sounds, I felt only a trust
that mirrored her own. Perhaps in the nature of
things, I was a mirror to her own perfect trust, and it
was she herself who worked the miracle. I don't know.

All I know is that in that fateful second my love
reached out to hold and embrace her. And in that moment the love I felt became so—there's not really a
word for it, but it seemed so—*comprehensive,* so complete and utterly fearless that the love may not have
been "mine" alone. It is possible, I theorized later,
that my human love may have served to prime the
pump, so to speak, for one much greater. All I can say
with certainty is that I remember feeling what may
have been the greatest love I had ever known.

My physical sense was of something within me,
something tangible reaching instantaneously out to
her—nothing so specific as what Carlos Casteneda has
described as "luminous fibers extending from a point
above the navel," but a similar sensation. I had a def-
inite sense of something within me reaching out to
hold her in the calm center of a perfect moment.

Time itself seemed to slow, and I think it more
than just *seemed to.*

There were physical indications that it actually
did. For example, as Delany began to fall, her skirt
did not blow above her waist as one would expect it

to under such conditions. Instead it puffed out like a parachute, much as Alice's dress is shown in illustrations of her descent down the famous rabbit hole. I have seen films, of course, where events were shown in slow motion, but this was the first and only time I witnessed what appeared to be a slowing of real time.

But the strangest part of it, and most difficult of all to explain, is *the heightened sense of the casual* that pervaded her entire descent. It all seemed so very ordinary. As a result of this (or possibly as its cause), her fall occurred in perfect calm, her emotions untroubled and at peace. From some source within me, I somehow knew that the greatest thing I could do for her during those moments was to remain equally calm.

The whole while the little girl fell—seeming to float from the top floor, through the middle floor, and on down into the basement—her unblinking eyes looked steadily into mine. Even long after she had come to rest on the discarded lumber scraps that littered the concrete floor, she continued to look up at me, the perfection of her trust never so much as flickering, her eyes not once leaving mine, nor mine hers. She showed not the slightest trace of anxiety, fear, or discomfort. Knowing she was unhurt, I too remained calm.

It was as if something had come over us, sealing the two of us for those few seconds in some altered interpretation of time and space where gravity yields to the currents of love.

As Delany sat there looking up at me, obviously unhurt and unafraid, I wanted to ask her what it had been like for her. Did she feel it, too, those magical moments when time had seemed to slow? Although I learned later that she had, there was no time to ask her just then, for at that very moment her mother appeared at the top of the ladder where Delany herself had appeared but a moment earlier.

With a strange, almost déjà vu sense of history repeating itself, I watched as Marilyn smiled a friendly greeting and immediately began telling me about something they had done that day. She never forgot the exact words I used to break to her the news of her daughter's fall—even years later she still sometimes kids me about them. In self-defense I can only say that, feeling such a deep sense of awe and solemnity at having just witnessed something truly miraculous—and knowing full well that Delany rested unhurt below—I was still immersed in the profound sense of calm that had characterized those unprecedented moments. Without thinking how unusual it might seem to another, I naturally waited until the first suitable opening in her remarks before I broke in, not too rudely I hoped, and said, pointing casually down the opening, "Uh, by the way, . . . Delany fell."

Marilyn took one startled look down the stairwell. Upon seeing her daughter, who moments before had preceded her up the ladder, now sitting far below on the basement floor, she let out an involuntary scream and headed immediately back down the ladder calling—

"George! George! Delany fell into the basement! Hurry!"

George responded instantly. Within seconds both he and Marilyn were in the basement. They wasted no time helping their daughter up and carrying her outside, where they discovered, much to their relief, that she was indeed unharmed.

Afterward that little voice—the same one I suspect I heard a few minutes ago—broke into my dominant thoughts of gratitude and relief to suggest that I had been more than just an instrument of this event.

But I heard echoes of the second temptation in its logic then, and I reject it again now.

The sunlit fork of this old tree is feeling mighty comfortable at the moment. To any beguiler with nothing better to do than suggest that I cast myself down, I would reply, "Why bother?" I could almost fall asleep here in this warm sunlight. Besides, there was urgency in Delany's predicament, and there is certainly none now in mine.

This oak had been growing here for a century already when Europeans first saw these mountains. Should it die during my lifetime I will check its rings to see how it fared its early years under French dominion, to learn if the summer of 1783—when it was ceded to Spain—was wet or dry. I doubt it even noticed being sold back to France again in 1800, just three years before Benjamin Franklin purchased it from Napoleon. It would have been tall enough to climb then, too, though history suggests this is probably not the main reason why Dr. Franklin bought it. Napoleon is said to have sweetened the deal by throwing in an expanse of land the size of western Europe.

Strange, to think that Europeans claimed to "own" this tree for nearly two hundred years before anyone of European ancestry so much as walked within a mile of it.

Leaning back into the rough comfort of its trunk, my body relaxes, releasing the stresses of the storm. As near as I dare, I approach sleep, enjoying that tranquil, alert-but-resting level of visibility that late-night drivers, and especially truck drivers, know only too well. That level of minimal alertness in which alpha, theta, and even occasional REM states are thoroughly enjoyed while the lower half of the retinas continue to feed vital information into the time-honored, auto-pilot program that prevents you from swerving too far to the right or to the left. Or in my case, from leaning too far, which actually would be pretty hard to do even if I were asleep, for this is a large branch I straddle and my position in it is quite secure. Of course I won't actually *sleep*, I'll just rest for a while and breathe deeply this content—deeper and fuller than any I have known in recent days.

While I would not want to make my decisions from a half-conscious state, semiconsciousness does have certain advantages. Because the mind is not so focused, one can review several topics at the same time. While some of my thoughts continue to mull over the question of how I will ultimately get down from here, others mull over the mulling itself—until by and by a light wind comes to disperse all thought, and for a long while I know only the overwhelming presence of the day.

Not until I notice the new position of the sun do I realize that time has passed.

Throughout my meditation, I have been watching an upper branch of this tree gesture, as it waves in the wind, to a hickory sapling growing off toward the southwest. For an instant it looks so like a finger that my half-closed eyes involuntarily open wide. Further out, the branch I'm straddling comes near enough to that little hickory that I could probably reach it when the wind next blows it near. If I could once grab hold of it, it shouldn't be too difficult to jump on over into the smaller tree.

Since this branch angles upward, I would be grabbing the sapling at a point maybe thirty-five feet above the ground. Hopefully I can climb down enough to guide the direction it will lean when I throw my weight. With luck it could just possibly lower me to the ground—or near enough to jump.

The thing to do now is to climb out on this branch and wait for the wind to blow the little hickory within reach. It takes longer than I expected to inch carefully outward on my belly along this upward-sloping branch until I reach my destination and pull myself to an upright position. The distance to the ground takes on new meaning as I am about to attempt this, but I've done enough roofing to keep my eyes from a second look down.

My next step is to take hold of the sapling when the wind blows it near. I don't have long to wait. A strong gust puts the whole forest of surrounding tree-tops in motion. As the hickory sways toward my soon-to-be-abandoned perch it feels as if the branch beneath me lunges to meet it. In one instantaneous motion I grab hold of the sapling and—*kids, don't try this at home*—make the quick leap over, learning promptly that in one important particular my calculations have been in error: I have no time to shinny down so much as an inch!

The second my weight hits the sapling it lurches to the north, which fortunately is uphill and nearer to the ground. Almost immediately I am horizontal and avoid rushing backward only by quickly releasing one leg to dangle, while automatically twisting my torso to the side. The move helps—for a tenth of a second.

As I feel myself turning upside down with the continuing momentum of the sapling's bend, instinctively I release my leg and am left hanging by only my hands. I retain a firm grip as amazingly—it's the damndest thing!—the tree actually lowers me to within inches of the forest floor. I let go, and even before my feet drop onto the welcome carpet of leaves, the accommodating little tree springs back, slightly, but not seriously, burning my hands.

I am stained with green and decorated with assorted forest debris, but glad, so glad, to be back on the ground. Each step upon the forest's soft, wet leaves brings such a welcome sense of homecoming, I squat for a moment to plunge hands, too, into the cool soil.

Before my eyes confirm it, my ears inform me that the waterfall's volume has increased during my absence. While today's rain was not enough to turn this seasonal creek into the raging river it becomes once or twice a year, it has nevertheless increased the flow of the water here to many times its prestorm volume. From the look of it, I would guess that two to two and a half inches of rain fell while I was up in that oak.

The water flowing over the fall, a mere trickle this morning, is now enough to shower beneath. Climbing down into the spring basin, I transform thought to deed and am met with a happy surprise. The water is warm. Apparently the field of sun-warmed rocks it crosses before tumbling over the edge here has had sufficient time to remove its chill. Tilting my head back to drink in the fresh, moss-flavored rainwater, all my senses share in the enjoyment.

Shower complete, I decide to discard my cutoffs for something warmer. From beneath the ledge I retrieve my backpack, withdraw jeans and flannel shirt, and quickly dress. It takes only a moment to climb the stone steps out of the basin. Standing in the warm sunlight on the limestone ledge above the spring, I glance down. And my eyes come to rest. Upon an ancient remnant of another world.

ON THE LEDGE ABOVE THE WATERFALL is a bowl-shaped depression in the rock where the ancient inhabitants of this area once ground their corn, using, as was their custom, a rounded stone as pestle. There is a similar mortar further down used during drier times. I have seen this bowl before, its white a striking contrast to the surrounding gray, lichen-covered rock. Obviously chiseled and smoothed by hands other than wind and rain, this bowl was here two decades ago when my stewardship of this land began. Indeed, it was created long, long before. Yet somehow in the sunlight of this still-early afternoon it looks but recently abandoned.

A dusting of sand in its bottom causes me to squint and look more closely, so much does it resemble cornmeal that could have been ground but an hour ago. And an hour as these rocks reckon time could contain a human generation in each of its minutes and still seem to pass quickly. For a moment I wonder if I have come late for breakfast. I wet the tip of my finger and touch the yellow sand, then taste it to be sure. No, no cornmeal today.

It is beautiful here, this open, rocky glade above the spring. The whole of the mossy limestone flat is surrounded by steep, upward-sloping hills of forest, which rise sharply to the north in a stretch of miniature cliffs that look as though they have been sculpted by the hand of some imaginative artisan. They are draped with luxuriant foliage this spring day, wreathed with white-flower crowns of multiflora roses and ringed with garlands of blue spiderwort bouquets that appear cool and happy, resting in the white-oak shade atop long, cornlike stems. *A Heaven. In a Wild Flower.*

A flash of white draws my gaze upward. Overhead a goshawk glides in silent serenity, her outstretched wings motionless against the infinite blue depths of the now-clear sky. As beautiful to the sky as the flower is to the soil, an elegant white band accentuates tail feathers that spread fanlike to nearly half the width of her wings. Where her tail feathers emerge from her body is a symmetrical snowflake pattern, followed by an intermediary range of solid bluish-gray that fades to a clear ring of white, as if moments before she took flight, each feather had been dipped in oils just to contrast the canvas of today's blue sky.

She glances down, sees me in the creek bed, and gives out a *ka-ka-ka* cry that for the second time today reminds me of a gull. Her wings show detailed patterns and designs, combining in the graceful sweep of their feathers an interweaving of parallel and perpendicular lines as meaningful no doubt to a reader of such things as life lines on any palm. Infinity lies in the graceful sweep of her wings; and eternity, too, I suspect, in more than a few of her hours.

The sun has warmed this still-damp world to a temperature that invites a walk among the pools above the spring. In front of me it illuminates a patch of fennel—that yellow-flowering, mustard-resembling herb whose tiny aromatic seeds make such excellent seasoning. Like fireworks exploring July Fourth night skies, each tiny shoot sends out sixteen slender stems that burst into bouquets of yet another sixteen smaller stems, each culminating in microscopic sprays of yellow flowers—

Instantly I leap backward as a garter snake slithers the twenty-some-odd inches of its black-and-yellow body across the sunlit stones before me. The speed of my reaction surprises me, but I am thankful that it kept me from stepping on the snake. I have no wish to harm it. And had it been a copperhead, that reaction would have spared me the agony of a bite seldom fatal but often nearly so (a copperhead is reputed to carry as much venom as a rattler).

Copperheads outnumber people in the Ozarks by such an extraordinary ratio that most of us hope we never learn just what it is. They are not only our most common snake, they are, in all probability, our most common animal. I killed thirty of them in the yard around our house the first summer we lived here, all within a few feet of our living area. The old homestead had not been lived in for years, and the snakes had grown accustomed to nesting under the house as well as in the nearby root cellar.

Despite their overwhelming population, Sherry and I would have made some attempt to coexist with these members of the pit viper family had it not been for our children—among them, six-month-old Fin, and two-year-old Becky. To children that young, a copperhead bite can sometimes be fatal.

All the same, neither my children nor my own precautionary nature was able to prevent my heart from melting the following spring when the copperheads put in their second annual appearance. It was painful to pin them down with a rake and behead them with a shovel, and I somehow could not bring myself to make a habit of it.

This second year there were not nearly so many around as there were the first, so I decided that rather than kill them, I'd relocate them. I continued to pin them down with the rake, but instead of decapitating them, I would grasp them at that point behind their heads which makes it impossible for them to bite. With the writhing trespasser in a firm grip, I would carry it out to the county road where our mailbox stood—just over a mile away—release it on the other side, check for letters, and walk back home. This was in the days before we had neighbors in that direction, so I had a clear conscience in depositing the snakes in what was then an unpopulated area.

There were few enough copperheads around that summer that I managed to continue this new policy of relocating those I found until they went back into hibernation that fall. But their numbers grew so during the following summers that I did not have time to keep taking two-mile round-trip hikes each time I found another. When I was not away doing carpentry work, we were putting in long days, often from sunrise until sunset, planting fruit trees, fencing, making necessary repairs on the house, and tending our nearly one-acre garden.

Both principle and the cost of fuel made me hesitant to use a truck to haul off a snake. But in the end I yielded to expediency, and we automated the process. After I had secured the offending copperhead, I'd climb into the passenger seat of our pickup, and Sherry would drive the bouncing, three-quarter-ton snake shuttle to the end of the road, where I would disembark, spit out the dust, and throw the snake off into the bushes.

During the slow, bumpy drive to the mailbox I would stroke the copperhead, speaking to it gently, and doing what I could to calm its fears. I was surprised at how warmly they responded. Usually by the time we were a few hundred yards down the dirt road, the copperhead in question would be coiled comfortably in my lap.

Of course there is still a noteworthy rush of adrenaline the moment you throw the snake into the brush. You do not want to throw it too far or too hard for fear of injuring it. On the other hand, you want to be damn sure you throw it far enough. A copperhead can move with lightning speed when it decides to strike. I have seen them many times striking at shovels and rakes before I got them into a proper grip. It is a sobering sight.

Yet always by the time I had brought these friendly animals to the end of our long driveway, I had established a bond of sorts. More than once on throwing them into the brush I felt that sort of sorrow one feels when parting with a friend, thinking to myself that given another occasion, under different circumstances, I would enjoy getting to know these creatures a little better.

Only later did I suspect that the snakes might have understood more of this silent sentiment than I realized, for many of them began returning. The first few times I caught a copperhead that looked familiar, I shrugged it off. Yet by the third or fourth time I spotted these returning brethren, it was clear they were the same snakes.

The casual way in which they sought to take up acquaintance right where they had left off confirmed that they were either extremely curious, extraordinarily friendly, or—it was an outside chance, but it was possible—they had come back for another truck ride.

Several of the returnees did spend a disproportionate amount of their time lingering in the vicinity of the old pickup; and once, at Clyde Elam's service station, an attendant who opened the hood of my truck

found himself eyeball-to-eyeball with a five-foot copperhead. That old pit viper had coiled himself happily around the distributor, and it was all I could do
to coax him off.

Familiarity breeds a certain tolerance. After four
years of carting off snakes to the end of the road (and
even further when we discovered them coming back),
when our sixth year began to turn over into spring
and I walked outside one evening to the shed where
we kept our refrigerator and spotted a copperhead
coiled beneath its open door, I reacted calmly, making a mental note to relocate it the next morning. Little did I know that this single act of omission would
initiate a cycle of coexistence that was to last for the
next three years.

Accepting the daily presence of poisonous snakes
in our lives now seems nearly as incomprehensible to
me as it must have to that unsuspecting family whose
visit brought the cycle to an abrupt end.

It all began with our gas refrigerator. Had it not
been for this ingenious mechanism, living as we were
without electricity, we would have had no means of
refrigeration during the long, hot, five-month Ozark
summers. Recreational vehicles have now made gas
refrigerators a bit more common, but back then in
the Ozarks they were as rare as hens' teeth and all
but unheard-of except in Amish communities or in
those few areas still beyond reach of the power lines.

Why, in our quest for simplicity, did we not just
dispense with refrigeration altogether? It is a good
question, but we all have certain blind spots. Knowing how important these can be, I've always made a
point to choose mine carefully, and thoughts of ozone
and freon and such things would conveniently slide
into oblivion each time the weather warmed.

Our first summer here we did get by without a refrigerator, but we would often spend ten, even twelve,
hours in the garden on days when the thermometer
hovered stubbornly above ninety degrees until well
into the evening. Even wearing no more than cutoff
jeans, I would become so hot and sopped with perspi-
ration that, had I sufficient equity, I would have
taken out a second mortgage on my soul for a glass of
something with ice cubes floating in it.

After much searching I located an old but working
Servel, which I bought for twenty dollars. With the
help of three stout, young Amishmen, we unloaded
the lead-heavy machine from the back of my pickup.
Next to the truck itself, the Servel was the most so-
phisticated piece of technology I owned—and the
greatest wonder our children had ever seen. Although
I have listened to many explanations of how gas refrigerators operate, to this day I am still unable to
comprehend how a hot jet of fire can produce ice. A
machine that actually does this is a wonder equal to
the Sphinx—and, as far as I'm concerned, a great
deal more useful.

We could not keep the propane-fueled refrigerator
in the house. It was too old to burn cleanly, and its
profusion of gas fumes was more than we cared for in
the kitchen. An old toolshed stood just behind the
house, and there I placed it, carefully leveling it on
concrete blocks to ensure the proper circulation of its
coolant. Occasionally a strong wind would blow out
the gas jet and I would have to relight it, but other
than that, it required little maintenance.

It was in early spring when the nights were still
cool that I spotted the copperhead beneath it. Recently out of hibernation, he apparently found comfort in the warmth of the Servel's gas jet. The

morning after I first spotted him, the young snake was nowhere to be found. I had a lot on my mind so I gave the matter no further thought until the following evening when I was carrying out the leftover milk from supper.

I set my kerosene lantern down and looked beneath the refrigerator. Sure enough, there he was. Well, I was tired, it was late, and I didn't want to fool with a copperhead by lamplight. The next morning he was gone again, and as time passed, one procrastination led to another.

Before long it became apparent that this fire-loving reptile lived beneath the floorboards of our house. Shortly before dark each night he would make his way toward the warmth of the refrigerator's bright blue flame. Soon we all got to watching him crawl out from under the house in the late twilight.

Once or twice as he almost got underfoot, I tried to command his respect, but he treated our family with a casual indifference. By the time that summer had passed, he had become a sort of well-respected pet.

When late in the spring of the following year we discovered two other copperheads coiled alongside him beneath the old Servel, we took it more or less in stride. They earned their keep by eliminating mice, and what with one thing or another I never got around to doing anything about them. They didn't bother us and we didn't bother them. I even looked upon their presence in our lives as a sort of spiritual discipline.

When walking across thirty feet of open yard to the outhouse in the dark, you are careful where you place your feet. Every sense bristles. You are alert from head to toe—even if you only hope to take a quick leak and get back into bed as quickly as possible. You have no choice in the matter. Such heightened consciousness is good for body and soul. While out there, alive, alert, and awake, you notice the moonlight and the stars in a way that sleepers with a bathroom in the house and no copperheads on the premises simply cannot comprehend.

Apparently the arrangement was good for the snakes as well. Their numbers steadily increased. By their third summer with us there was, as our son Fin put it, "a whole mess of 'em."

The copperheads had become such matter-of-fact aspects of our existence, among ourselves we rarely mentioned them. In fact they were the furthest thing from my mind the day the visitors from Findhorn arrived.

They hailed from a community in the north of Scotland that we had first heard of in a book called *The Secret Life of Plants.* The community's interests were similar to our own, and our correspondence had led to this visit. It was our guests' first evening with us, and long after dark we were sitting at the kitchen table deep in conversation.

Now, you would think that when our twelve-year-old happened across so unusual a spectacle in the yard, he would have possessed the sensitivity to quietly take me aside and discreetly whisper his news. Not Bill. With the fanfare of a circus ringmaster, he threw open the door and announced with undisguised joy—

"Dad, come quick, there's a bunch of huge copperheads all coiled around each other right by the door of their tent!"

Suddenly the woman who I thought had come from the north of Scotland announced that she hailed from Los Angeles—a city girl who had never before seen a snake in the wild, let alone a writhing mass of poisonous ones between her and her sleeping bag in the dark.

Until that moment I don't think that we had ever really seen our living situation through someone else's eyes.

Less than a week earlier an incident had occurred that should have alerted me to the fact that things were getting out of hand. I had begun to sit down in an old rocking chair we kept out on the front porch. Just as I was in the process of lowering into it that portion of my anatomy for which chairs are designed, I glanced down and saw one of our copperheads coiled on the seat. It had been a close call. The resulting bite would not have been in the leg, but in a juncture of legs. I did not relish the thought.

Now, with this latest incident, I could no longer deny the facts. Our visitors were traveling with small children, unfamiliar with forest living; it was not fair to subject them to such risk. The snakes were becoming altogether too friendly; it was possible someone would get seriously hurt unless I killed them. So I did. But I am still not convinced that I did the right thing. You never know about such decisions. You just have to do what you think is best at the time and try not to feel too guilty about it afterward.

Yet these gentle, brown-camouflaged snakes have never harmed me in any way, and I am grateful that it has now been many years since I have faced the necessity of killing another.

Recently, walking barefoot through the fields, Valarie stepped on a copperhead. "Felt cool and soft," she said.

The snake merely glanced up with mild annoyance, seeming to realize it was an accident and willing to forgive the oversight. Becky later did the same thing. She, too, was barefoot at the time, and this snake's reaction was identical to the other's. It may have been the girls' bare feet that communicated to the snakes the fact that they were in no danger. If those copperheads had been stepped on by booted heels, things may have not turned out so well.

While I have been enjoying my recollections of what may well have been the only domesticated *au naturel* copperheads in history, I have been wading through the ankle-deep water of the Western Sea with hopes of catching a glimpse of my old flute-loving water moccasin acquaintance. But again, I see no sign of him.

Spotting him could be difficult. If a water moccasin senses danger, he will keep his body beneath the surface of the water, with only a trace of eyes and nostrils showing. I've often watched them swimming across a river or a pool; if you do not know what to look for, it's easy to mistake one for a branch floating innocently by.

Suddenly a loud crashing sound comes from the brush behind me. As I spin quickly around, something brushes up against my foot. My adrenals feel a bit foolish when I see only a small lizard darting through the leaves and a murky, half-decayed leaf alongside my foot.

AN AVENUE OF AFTERNOON SUNLIGHT leads me
back to the First Rocks, past the moss-covered stones
that fork at the pool's edge, and on into their eastern
heart, near the chinkapin where the lizards were.
Here the width of the open area narrows to but a few
yards and is bordered on the north by a long, low,
brush-concealed cave. I look for the collareds, but the
chinkapin is shaded now, and the lizards have probably moved onward with the sun.

Before I can check the impulse, my eyes have
found the nearest distinct shadow, assessed its angle
in relation to north, and estimated the time at around
3:00 P.M. Nothing wrong with this, but the fact that
the calculation was involuntary bothers me for a moment. I would have preferred to have been consulted,
I think—then laugh in spite of myself.

If I am to have a goal today at all, what better one
than to accept the awareness I have in each moment,
trusting that it is just what the moment requires—no
more, no less. Enlightenment itself holds to no arbi-
trary standard; its awareness flows like water around
time and circumstance, seeking the optimal level of
exchange, interacting creatively with all it encounters.
The awareness that nature provides is not always
what I want or think it should be, yet it's always what

I need to take care of what's right in front of me. Now, if I can just remember that tomorrow.

Where the cave across from the chinkapin begins—before it widens and becomes large enough to sit beneath in the heat of a summer's day—a small spring moistens the rocks, dripping regularly throughout all but the driest months. I never thought much of this little spring until I once made the mistake of rolling out my sleeping bag on the dry rocks below it, only to discover that our local animals take it quite seriously. It soon became apparent that I had placed myself in the direct path to their watering hole.

It didn't bother me too much as twilight fell. While sitting absolutely motionless here, I was able for several long minutes to observe a flock of wild turkeys from less than six feet away. But soon after the darkness had become too complete to see anything but stars and the occasional satellite, I heard some large creature ambling casually toward the spring, snapping large branches beneath its paws.

The deer are never so careless, and that did not leave too many other possibilities. I knew only that I was between "it" and the place where it was accustomed to drinking. And "it" could very well be a bear.

Although the last of our indigenous bears disappeared in the early 1960s, the Conservation Department has been releasing them in remote wooded areas like this—here a bear, there a bear—gradually reintroducing them to this part of the Ozarks. And they seem to be succeeding.

Not long ago a black bear treed a man right in the middle of Summersville, our nearest town. Bud Cooley, an experienced woodsman, was trying to herd the animal out of the town's park before somebody shot it. But the herder quickly became the herded, and even after Bud had made it up into the tree, the six-foot bear charged it several times, leaping up, trying to get him down. Bud said he judged the bear was an adult because its molars were all worn down.

"Got a real close look at 'em," he said.

This was probably not the same black bear that walked boldly down the main street of Willow Springs a few years back, not because it couldn't easily have ranged this far, but because that particular bear weighed in at over seven hundred pounds. While these incidents were funny at the time, their humor escaped me as I recalled them while lying there between the "thing" and its drink.

The other possibility, of course, was that it might be a mountain lion.

As far as I know, Sherry and our daughter Becky were the last people to see a native Ozark mountain lion in this area—and that was twenty years ago. It happened just a few months after we had moved into the old farmhouse, which like the miles of forest around it had been uninhabited for many years. Sherry and two-year-old Becky were walking up the hill toward our yard when between them and the house they saw a large yellow cat with a long, yellow tail.

"It was about the size of a German shepherd," Sherry said. "Right there at the edge of the yard."

I might have thought they had seen only a bobcat, an animal fairly common in these parts; but bobcats are gray and noted for their short, stubby, almost nonexistent tails. Also, bobcats tend to be considerably smaller.

This was hardly a cheering thought as "the creature" continued to crash toward me. Nor was it the best time to recall a place called "Panther Springs," just a couple of miles away as the crow flies. Or—

I thought as I heard the snap of another large branch—as the cat stalks.

"Yo!" I hollered, sitting up in my sleeping bag and making as much noise as I could. The unidentified cruncher froze. And although I lay there in the darkness afterward and watched the same satellite go by twice—which meant that about four hours had passed—I did not hear so much as another leaf crunch. However, I obviously was not sleeping well, so after certain thoughtful considerations I moved my sleeping bag to a less traveled area.

The area to the south of this seasonal spring is truly magical. Despite the relatively small amount of ground that it covers, I count it one of the most spectacular works of nature in this vicinity. What it lacks in grandeur of scale it makes up for in detail.

Much of that detail takes shape in the cave, which below the spring gradually widens until its opening expands from three feet to a comfortable six. From the creek bed the strata of rock that forms its ceiling is visible for several feet before it merges upward into the hillside. Over its entire length, a thick mass of sagegrass tumbles in long strands, the color of blond hair. Sprinkled throughout the blond are the bright orange flowers of the honeysuckle. The entire sage-honeysuckle mass droops down to meet witch hazel and hawthorn bushes growing up from below, effectively concealing the cave from casual view. Where its ceiling first opens to standing height, the bushes do permit human passage, but one has to be careful. Poison ivy grows liberally among the hawthorn.

With care I enter and make myself comfortable on one of several seat-high blocks of stone. Looking back out into the vibrant floral world I've just left, it feels as though I'm in some nether region, for not much grows here where the sun never reaches, though there is a bit of moss and lichen.

Behind my stone seat are numerous declivities—curious moss-speckled nooks containing the dripping forms of miniature stalactites, which despite their modest size must nonetheless count their age in centuries. These nooks would make convenient niches for a candle some stormy night, providing light, if not much warmth, for a straggler who might choose to shelter here, though if the storm were to continue long, he or she would be wise to move on. After a heavy rain the water will nearly fill this cave.

This seasonal flooding requires about twice the rainfall we had today and usually occurs not more than a couple times a year. One year, however, this creek flooded four times, the last on Christmas Day. As I look out I can still see an oak limb that was washed downstream in that storm. It, and a four-foot pile of debris, remain lodged against the pair of walnut trees where they came to rest when the waters subsided.

Using the cave as my roadway into the mysterious "wood between the worlds" that separates the First Rocks from the spring, I emerge from beneath the ledge, wishing the leaves did not crunch so loudly beneath my feet. Here, where the look is distinctly more wild and formidable than in the open rocky areas on either side of it, the air, indeed the whole forest, is utterly still, and I have no wish to frighten away what creatures may inhabit this silent wonderland—or almost silent.

A quiet humming pervades the air. Looking upward, I locate its source high up in a white oak. I see now where that branch I noticed lodged downstream originally grew. It must have been hollow before it detached from the tree. Where it has broken off there now extends a tube a foot and a half in diameter, open at its end and quite alive with bees. From here poison ivy prevents a direct approach, but later I'll approach it by way of the path to the spring and have a closer look at those bees.

The rock ledge above the cave from which I've just emerged widens as the cave narrows until its eastern end fades into a cliff of bare rock, about eight feet from top to bottom and weathered into distinct facial features. My back against a scarlet oak, I settle cross-legged among the leaves to see what thoughts these stony countenances inspire this afternoon.

There is a sense of presence that seems to linger near these faces. Their features are never twice the same. Like ours, they change with the passage of hours, days, seasons, and with the passage of the years. Which of their aspects are emphasized at any given moment depends on the angle of sunlight, the amount of surrounding foliage, and how much of the rock that forms them is darkened by water dripping from above.

These subtle shifts bring out an ever-changing range of expression in the eyes and sober mouths of these limestone faces. Some days they look benign, some days angry, other days happy or sad. Just as we alter our expressions with the muscles available to us, their expressions alter with angles of sunlight and changes in moisture and vegetation.

Here and in similar places native peoples communed with the spirits of the earth, the spirits of stone, the spirits of these ancient mountains. My own experiences here have led me to believe that where such features exist, and where there has been a tradition of human association with them, the spirit world is more accessible than in locations where little or no exchange has occurred. When one approaches such a place in reverence and openness, the earth, it seems, will occasionally give certain gifts. Gifts that can take many forms. Sometimes they come as telepathic understandings. Sometimes as visions or premonitions.

Formations like these have been known to foretell earthquakes such as the New Madrid quakes of 1811 and 1812. Centered just a hundred miles from here, these quakes, estimated between 8.4 and 8.6 on the Richter scale, are said to have been the most powerful in U.S. history, buckling streets in Washington, D.C., and ringing church bells as far away as Boston and Philadelphia. Yet the tribes living near those eastern cities, as well as the tribes of the central plains, had been warned of the quakes weeks in advance by the Shawnee prophet Tecumseh.

Our history upon this mysterious world records countless instances of such prophecies. Dreams, visions, premonitions whose accuracy was proven by subsequent events, and which often, like Tecumseh's prediction of the New Madrid quakes, saved thousands of lives. The more I learn of such things—and of how common they have been as far back as our records go—the more I wonder at the modern world's apparent disinterest in the invisible realm from which they come.

Aboriginal societies have traditionally given the invisible (or spirit) world as much importance as the physical. Yet in the West we have only recently begun to recognize its importance. The scientific advances of this century have taught us that the behavior of matter, energy, light, gravity, and even time cannot be explained without reference to the portion of the invisible world that we have identified as the fabric of time and space. Yet it has many facets, and these manifest differently as they touch upon various

fields of human study. While we have come to recognize its role in many of these fields—and now see it as
central to our understanding of everything from the
spiraling of the galaxies to the play of subatomic par-
ticles—we have yet to recognize its role in a field of
far more practical relevance.

Just as twentieth-century physics was born and
raised on a new understanding of the invisible world's
role in physical events and processes, many now feel
that it is only a matter of time until something com-
parable to a theory of relativity transforms the field
of biology with an outline of the invisible world's role
in relation to living organisms. Some biologists are
now speculating that it may soon prove as important
to our understanding of biology as it has become to
our understanding of physics. Others go so far as to
suggest that it may even hold the key to understanding the life force itself, which, despite extraordinary
advances in our understanding of biology's mechan-
ics, remains as much a mystery to us today as it was
to our ancestors thousands of years ago.

For nearly a decade, leading-edge researchers have
been quietly gathering evidence to support the theory that life-forms originate in an invisible dimension
of high-energy fields. In that dimension each creature
retains a vibrational blueprint that interpenetrates
its body and is the source of its body's life. When a
life-form embodies this blueprint, it serves the purpose for which nature brought it into being; it is
healthy and affects its environment positively. When
a life-form does not embody its blueprint, it fails to
serve nature's purpose, is unhealthy, and affects its
environment negatively.

The species of the vegetable realm, as I have come
to understand them, are relatively accurate embodi-
ments of nature's intentions. Animal species, on the

other hand, are given a far broader range of choices, and they do not always choose to evolve along pathways in harmony with their environments. Yet overall, animals achieve what nature intends.

In creating insects, fishes, amphibians, reptiles, birds, and mammals—and by giving them the freedom to modify their bodies and the ways they use them more rapidly than plants—nature was able to greatly accelerate evolution. However, by about 2 million years ago—some 350 million years after air-breathing creatures first appeared on the land—evolution hit a ceiling.

To break through it, a new type of creature was required.

Of all the earth's species, our race has been given the greatest behavioral latitude, the greatest freedom of choice. From nature's perspective this makes us potentially the most useful of all the species. No other creature has a greater capacity to assist this world's continuing biological development. Yet the same intellects that enhance our capacity to create increase our ability to destroy.

Why did nature take such a gamble?

My own feeling is that the earth requires a species like ours to fully develop her potential. Without human beings to introduce a more focused type of precision creativity, evolution may be unable to break on through into that next—and, I believe, long-awaited—stage in which a tool-making, language-speaking species understands nature's goals and realizes that it is in its own best interests to help bring them about.

Without the current environmental crisis it is possible that we might never have looked up long enough from our primitive territorial games to notice that we face an opportunity of metahistoric proportions, an opportunity that if accepted could well prove a milestone in our human development as significant as the acquisition of language.

If we accept this opportunity, our species would become the first to consciously participate in the earth's evolutionary processes, thereby initiating an unprecedented new era of planetary development—a second phase of evolution that would use the first as a springboard into a whole new order of organic unfoldment. Such an evolutionary breakthrough would activate new systems and introduce new energies that could, over a relatively short period of time, bring planetary transformations as revolutionary as those the human body experiences at puberty.

Sitting with my back against this scarlet oak, acorn remnants scattered about, an analogy comes to mind. This tree records its genetic information in the tiny germ of an acorn and leaves it with a dormant spark of time-released energy. When activated, that tiny spark of life unleashes the awesome power of the full-grown tree. The essence-germ breaks through its acorn shell, sprouts into a sunlit world, and enters a realm of new and previously inconceivable possibility. It grows from a sphere the size of a pebble to a tree like the Conference Oak, which can shade beneath it a hundred people on a sunny day.

Could we be the essence-sprouts of nature's genius; what the acorn is to the oak—to the intelligence that took a planet once as lifeless as the moon and made it what it is today? I believe that nature's power is now urging us from within, even as multiplying crises urge us from without, challenging us to crack through history's shell, to break through our myopic assumptions and open our minds to a far deeper understanding of this world.

Human cooperation centered on the earth's evolutionary purposes seems to generate a kind of energy, an increase in vitality. This could be the energy that will finally allow us to operate our body-mind circuitry at full capacity. Without it, we may be no more effective than 120-volt circuits limping along on 12 volts of current. We are now able to make use of only a small percentage of the human brain's incredible capacity. Most of us find it difficult to wake up enough to piece together why we are here. Our historical mistake has been to turn to religion, to culture, to government—to human institutions—for explanations of who we are, what this world is, and what our lives here mean.

Why not look to nature?

In the makeup of the shrubs, wildflowers, and trees growing near these weather-carved faces in the cliffstone, I can identify the cooperative interplay of many formative influences. The four forces of the ancient alchemists—water, air, earth, and fire—have all left signatures here, written in the mergings, mixtures, and blendings of their prodigy. Hydrogen, oxygen, carbon, molecules, minerals, microbes—and agencies too numerous to mention—must all cooperate to produce the life I see before me. Each of them contributes something so vital, so essential to the whole, that were any one of them removed this land would support not a single form of life—not even so much as a single cell. The extent of this collaboration is far more than I can comprehend, but I have seen enough to recognize the obvious—

This forest is built not upon the struggle that many still associate with the concept of evolution. It is built upon the genius of cooperation.

I have no argument with so practical a strategy as the survival of the fittest. But the long record of evolutionary experimentation reveals something that has only recently begun to get the attention it deserves: The fittest are the most cooperative.

Jonas Salk, inventor of the polio vaccine, has suggested replacing the term "survival of the fittest" with "survival of the wisest." But *survival of the most cooperative* strikes me as a term better still, and I have a feeling Dr. Salk would not too vehemently disagree. He and others more scientifically qualified than I are showing that our human survival now depends not on our further subjugation of nature, but on our greater cooperation within the natural order.

My skepticism prevents me from being an atheist. It requires more faith than I can muster to believe that a world as exquisitely engineered as ours came into being without intelligent participation somewhere along the line. I guess my mind just isn't urban enough to grasp the concept of an accidental forest; and I have never been able to get past that one initial block to consider accidental oceans and biospheres, accidental eyes and ears, accidental lives. In places where cycles of commerce loom larger than the cycles of the moon or the cycles of the seasons, there are those, of course, who believe such things, but native peoples know better. And people close to the land.

10

HERE IN THE HEART of the hollow, among the thick growth of this wood between the worlds and its faces of stone, it is not advisable to remain motionless too long. It gives the insects a false impression.

They assume that whatever spirit may have once motivated your flesh has relinquished its claim and left its former territory open for settlement. Soon you begin to feel an assortment of malnourished, six-legged carnivores creeping up your legs, crawling down your neck, and in other ways drawing your attention to the fact that nature does not particularly favor the idle. As my left eyelid is penetrated by the proboscis of some hungry insect, I recall a reason for moving on.

The bee colony I noticed in the nearby oak, the tree we call the Gnome Oak, may be an old hive relocated from another tree, possibly the same one whose honey once fueled us through a winter of granola-sweetened mornings. Eager to have another look at it, I make my way back through the cave, determined not to comment on, inspect, or poke fingers into its endless crevices.

Reemerging into the sunlight, I set a brisk pace across the rocks, but I've barely reached the little pool when I suddenly find myself the subject of a blue jay's outrage. He scolds me furiously from the branches of the butternut, looking down at me and gesturing accusingly with his beak. I pause and look up, mouth agape, wondering what I could have possibly done to offend him.

The rain has left the air remarkably clear. The sky behind the butternut is a blue as deep as the color of the jay's feathers. He looks almost like a little piece of sky himself up there among the green leaves. Abruptly his screeching stops, and I pause to appreciate the streaks of white along his wings. Overhead a lone wood duck hurries to some northward destination. I wonder what could be so urgent—then I remember. I, too, had forgotten.

The journey is as important as the destination. I take a deep breath, and once more I am standing in the presence of a perfect day. As I lower my eyes back to the jay, he shifts uncomfortably, as if wondering what had just come over him, then suddenly flies off to the south, leaving me staring at the butternut—a strange and puzzling tree.

Its trunk shows more pileated woodpecker holes than I can count. Some are perfectly round, others, oblong. But for each current woodpecker hole there are several circular domes that give every indication of having been former holes that the tree has somehow healed. I am told this is not theoretically possible. I wonder if this butternut knows that?

With all its woodpecker penetrations and insect colonies, one would think this tree could not survive more than another season or two. Yet I remember it virtually unchanged for fifteen years. Each spring it awakens as robust and vibrant as the last. This is something of a miracle in the middle of a creek bed whose periodic flooding often sends powerful torrents of water rushing through here three or four feet in depth.

Trees everywhere develop features characteristic of the terrain around them, but this immediate area seems to have more than its share. Not far from the butternut is another tree every bit as remarkable.

A white oak grows a few yards up the hill, on a spot that must have seen considerable erosion since it was a sapling. Its upper roots can be seen coiling downward from well above the ground. Like many of the trees this early in May, it is not yet fully awake. A yellow tinge still lightens the green of its leaves, and it retains its small, orange flowers. Ten feet above the ground, its largest branch meets the trunk at the exact angle of a mammoth arm bent at the elbow. Just above where the branch makes its right angle upward, a smaller branch (about three inches in diameter) grows toward it from the tree's main trunk. When it reaches the branch that forms the upraised arm, instead of continuing in the normal way of branches, the smaller branch merges right into the larger.

The result is a near-perfect triangle of living wood halfway up the tree, a handsome representation of one of nature's primary forms and a profound example of her ingenuity. The triangle serves the practical purpose of helping to support the weight of the arm-like branch as it extends out over the First Rocks, support that it has apparently been providing for some time, for the branch has grown much larger than it could have without it.

As the gnarled old Gnome Oak glides into view, my vision zeros in on the rough-textured series of mounded burls from which it derives its name. It is the largest and most strangely shaped growth I have ever seen on any tree—a waist-high mass that doubles the diameter of an already sizable tree that must be nearly three hundred years old. The massive burl bears an uncanny resemblance to the face of a sober but not unfriendly gnome.

Looking up at the hollow stub where the bees have made their home, I see hundreds, if not thousands, of the tireless little creatures buzzing about the opening. There must be many times that number inside. A few of the bees returning with their cargo pause at the hive's entrance long enough to explain to those departing where the best nectar can be found. Through an extraordinarily rapid series of aerial gymnastics they trace diagrams in the air that tell the others exactly how to reach certain fields. These aerial maps are so precise they can successfully guide a young worker bee setting out on her first flight to a specific bush—often miles away.

Once again I find myself thinking of our son Bill. A carpenter now in St. Louis, on one of his recent visits he borrowed my chain saw and bold as you please felled the hollow tree that I suspect was this hive's previous home. To his (and to his practical-minded Ozark siblings') delight, he succeeded in stealing a bountiful cache of wild forest honey. Much as I appreciate honey, this did not sit well with me, as I had often visited that hive, listening to their industrious drone, and intuiting the collective mind that organizes them much like a single entity.

When I expressed my dissatisfaction, Bill just grinned and handed me a slice of bread dripping with honey, asking if I didn't agree it was the best we'd ever had. I had never tasted better. As my objectivity blurred over with a second mouthful, and I sliced another piece of Jessie's homemade bread in preparation for more, it occurred to me that I had told Bill that he was welcome to cut standing deadwood. And it didn't take much guesswork to figure out who had taught him to stretch a point.

This Gnome Oak is but one of many trees throughout the thousand acres of forest between here and the Jacks Fork River that have become personally meaningful to me over the years. Some are as individually adaptive as the pileate-sculpted butternut, others as uniquely creative in their forms of expression as the white oak with its triangle of living wood. Toward many of them I feel a quality of affection not all that different from what I feel toward the people closest to me in this life.

"Whole thing's gonna be clear-cut," a neighbor stopped by to tell me one afternoon. "Just thought you oughta know. It's all being sold to one of them big logging outfits."

Unfortunately this proved to be more than a rumor. I soon verified that most of the land between our home and the river (two miles away) was in the process of being sold to a logging firm, which intended to clear-cut it. There was no decision involved. Sherry and I knew ourselves well enough to know that we'd do everything in our power to protect the forest and the trees we loved.

We had no idea how thoroughly this would change our lives and the lives of so many who are now residents of this area.

Working closely with our neighbors Patti and Terry Turowski, my brother Tom, and Sherry's sister Eileen, we came up with a plan.

Our idea was simple: Stall off the loggers by offering the owner a slightly higher price for the property, secured by a small down payment, then raise the purchase money for the entire tract by selling a third of it to people who wanted to see the trees protected. The third that we proposed to sell would be divided into five- and ten-acre parcels covered by environmental restrictions. The remaining two-thirds would be owned in common and preserved as a wilderness area.

The only problem with this idea was that when we pooled our resources, the six of us found that we had less than $100 among us; and the cost of the land ran well into to the six-figure range. We did some rough calculating and concluded that the smallest down payment the owner would likely accept in exchange for holding off sale to the loggers for six months was $5,000—just over 2 percent of the purchase price— and we'd be lucky if he'd accept that. We decided the $5,000 would be our sign. If the project was meant to be, somehow it would turn up. Two days before the property was to be sold to the loggers, a woman called (no one we knew) and said she had heard of what we were trying to do and was sending a friend over that afternoon with the $5,000 we needed to put our plan into operation.

Nine months later we had raised nearly a quarter of a million dollars. And had purchased the property.

Today the land owned by the Greenwood Forest Association and its members—over a thousand acres— is the site of a thriving environmental community. Windmills, solar panels, and a variety of energy-efficient, soft-tech homes rest among the once-threatened trees. The initiative took three years to complete, for even after we had purchased the land we still needed to finish selling all the parcels—and I did not feel free to turn over leadership of the association until enough of the owners had moved here to assure that it would be responsibly managed.

When I envisioned the project and drafted its initial literature, I had assumed that we would be able to raise a sizable percentage of the necessary purchase funds through donations from conservationists and organizations whose purpose is the preservation of the environment. I was wrong. And for a reason that had never occurred to me.

Conservationists objected to our project because people would someday live on a portion of the land. They held to a belief that I have since found prevalent among many in the environmental movement: that people by their very nature harm the land they live upon.

This is another of those quintessentially urban attitudes that wouldn't last through half a summer of organic gardening. It ignores the fundamental issues of resource utilization and lifestyle at the core of our environmental problems and shifts the focus to sentimental legislation that soothes the national (consumer) conscience with a pretense of preservation—a pretense because industry has such a positive genius for circumventing it that much of it isn't worth the paper it's printed on. The leasing of our local Mark Twain National Forest to lead-mining interests is a case in point.

Our challenge is not to fence off portions of the earth to protect them from our destructive lifestyles; it is to explore lifestyles that allow us to *improve* the places where we live.

There is nothing inherent in our race that makes us despoilers of the environment. Our capacity to enhance this world is infinitely greater than our capacity to destroy. We need wilderness areas, to be sure, but far more than vast tracts of land where humans are denied—or sprawling national forests where gathering firewood is illegal but large-scale mining and timber harvesting is not—we need places of balance.

Our hope was to create a loose-knit community setting based on shared ecological values that would actively encourage people to reduce their consumption, produce as much as possible of what they consumed, and minimize the income they needed to make up the difference. Our vision was idealistic enough to inspire the necessary lifestyle changes in the people who chose to participate in it, but fortunately it was not so idealistic that it failed to work.

We knew that if fault for the practice of clear-cutting could be laid on any doorstep, that doorstep was far from these Ozark Mountains. By that point in my life I had worked side by side with many a former logger. I knew that neither they nor the owners of our local sawmills typically earned much more than what was required to meet expenses and provide for the needs of their families. The profit from the clear-cutting of our hardwood forests is accrued by urban industries that rely on the flow of cheap resources from the country.

So when I made my presentation to Mountain View's chamber of commerce, I didn't criticize the local timber industry. I simply pointed out that our proposed method of "using" that particular tract of land would, during its first three years alone, bring into the local economy ten to fifteen times more revenue than if the land were stripped of its trees.

The media picked up on this. Our regional newspaper, the *West Plains Quill,* started things off with photographs of the area and a page-one story that quickly led to supportive editorials in the *Kansas City Star* and the *St. Louis Post Dispatch.* A chain reaction of favorable coverage ensued. Articles and editorials appeared in national magazines; television stations flew in their crews; and the prime-time documentary that appeared on NBC news resulted in a flood of letters and more calls than our four-party phone line could accommodate.

Yet while all these factors contributed to making our Greenwood Forest Project a reality, the vision behind it was born of something deeper. At times it seemed to those of us at the core of the project almost a kind of magic.

Midnight. Ann Arbor, Michigan. A snowstorm has me stranded at the bus station. I recognize a voice across the room. Surprised, I look up to see a leading Missouri environmentalist who is running for congress in our home district. The next day during our ride home he helps me draft environmental guidelines to govern the use of the parcels we hope to sell.

A man who owns a cabin a few yards from our favorite swimming hole turns out to be a lawyer with a top St. Louis law firm. The firm offers to do all our legal work—free if our efforts fail, at a charity rate if we succeed.

Chance meetings. Bizarre coincidences. Last-minute financial help. The project was characterized by enough unusual incidents to fill a small volume. Yet for me one stands out above all others. It occurred shortly after we learned that the forest was slated for clear-cutting and inspired my writing of the project's initial brochure.

Late one evening under a full moon Sherry and I were walking along the many old and forgotten trails that crisscrossed the threatened land. Every now and then we'd stop in a grove of older trees to offer a prayer or simply to stand silently among them for a while. Two o'clock in the morning found us sitting high upon a ridge overlooking the Jacks Fork River in a grove of old-growth trees that included some of Missouri's few remaining virgin pines.

Sherry was meditating at the base of one of these ancient trees. A few yards away I was sitting at the base of another, the tallest in this particular stand.

Not long into my meditation I made a shift in position and leaned back against the tree's trunk. As I did, my center of awareness seemed to detach from my body. Like a pebble dropping into a well, I felt myself falling into the depths of its being. The falling continued until I experienced what I can only describe as a kind of splash and an instantaneous surge upward into the tree's branches, needles, and cones, as though the tree had suddenly become an extension of my own sensory organs. Whether the subsequent impressions I received were those that the tree regularly experienced or due to some unusual juxtaposition of our respective forms of awareness, I can't say. But I know what I experienced.

I sensed the surrounding expanse of forest-covered hills as if they were my own skin, feeling upon them the presence and movement of bobcat, deer, possum, turkey, beaver, and other creatures within the mile or two region that this tree had somehow brought within me. Like an artery delivering oxygen to constituent cells, I felt the river below breathing energy upward into the moonlit air.

While simultaneously experiencing myself as both the tree and the human being sitting at its base, I also experienced myself—in a way that is difficult to convey verbally—as if I *were* the surrounding river valley.

A vision came to me in which I saw what was clearly that same moonlit valley, covered with a forest of magnificent conifers, trees whose trunks were many feet in diameter and whose tops disappeared high above. Fifty yards or more separated each of these enormous trees, leaving among them open areas that admitted sun, sky, wind, and rain. In these open areas beneath, between, and among the larger trees grew oaks, birches, hickories, walnuts, smaller pines, and other tree species that I was unable to identify.

The vision continued. Loggers entered the grove and proceeded to harvest most of the smaller trees, leaving only the towering conifers and a few of the midsized ones, which apparently had been selected to replace the mature trees when their spirits did eventually choose to move onward, as it was clear in time they would. How the loggers determined which trees to harvest and which to leave behind I never learned, but it came to me all at once and I somehow knew that the smaller trees were being given by the larger to serve our planet in meeting the needs of her people. Through the larger trees it seemed that the earth had set up a field of energy, a radiant grid of vibration involving some kind of bioelectrical current that caused the younger, smaller trees to thrive.

When I saw the loggers harvest these oaks, walnuts, and hickories, it amazed me, for they were the size of some of the largest trees that grow in these Ozark forests today. Until I saw human figures among them, I had not realized the full scale of the massive conifers—a type of redwood?—which towered over all. As I watched I had the strange impression that the larger trees were creating vibrational patterns that stimulated the growth of the younger trees, causing them to grow far more rapidly than they would without such assistance.

Later, while telling Sherry of this vision, she said it reminded her of something a physicist had once told us. The physicist had described a dramatic moment that occurred one day in the darkroom while she was developing a Kirlian photograph of a leaf bud. As she lifted the dripping print from the developing fluid and watched it slowly take shape before her eyes, she saw there in the intensified, electrically charged field around the bud the entire skeletal structure of the leaf-to-be! There it was—something invisible revealed, the complete blueprint into which the bud would grow.

When a group of us gathered in Nottingham a few years ago to help film a British television series on this and related phenomena, biochemist Rupert Sheldrake spoke of these invisible formative patterns as morphogenetic fields, fields that facilitate processes of formation: atomic, subatomic, molecular, cellular. Apparently it is a phenomenon that has been detected at virtually every level of organization. (Rupert's book *A New Science of Life* describes the phenomenon in scientific detail that supports the work of others like physicist David Bohm. Bohm's book *Wholeness and the Implicate Order* takes a broader view, postulating the existence of an invisible universe into which the visible universe is slowly—to use my term—blooming.)

My vision that night suggested that the larger trees were doing something along these lines, creating some kind of morphogenetic field that facilitated the growth of the younger, smaller trees, which were then periodically harvested.

Yet even as I watched, I realized that to get from here to there would require a major leap of faith. Not until those larger trees were in existence, indeed, not until they had matured, would we ever see the prolific results of their capacity to create the conditions that allowed for this type of accelerated growth. To witness the beginnings of this phenomenon (or, for that matter, even to have tangible evidence of its existence) we would first have to establish and implement—perhaps for as long as a century or more—forestry practices quite different from those we currently employ.

The vision also seemed to imply that although many mature groves already exist—in national forests, parks, wilderness preserves, and other areas—this phenomenon does not occur without human participation. It requires the involvement of people who can access the currents of consciousness that animate a forest, conversing with the trees and evoking their participation. (I also sensed that somewhere people are already pioneering this work, and that before long I would likely run across a report of their progress.)

Although I had previously suspected it, my experience that night beneath the virgin pine convinced me that mature trees are intelligent life-forms whose cooperation can be solicited, much as Luther Burbank solicited the cooperation of plants, developing many of the new and superior varieties of flowers and vegetables that today grow in virtually every backyard garden.

At first I was hesitant to mention this experience to the others who shared our hopes of saving the forest, but at Sherry's encouragement, shortly after receiving the project seed money, I did. As subsequent events proved, I had underestimated our friends. Not only were they quite supportive, it turned out that Patti and Terry had been interested in such things for years. In fact it was Terry who encouraged me to explore the possibility of communication with other trees, suggesting that some ongoing exchange might help us in our efforts to save the forest.

With the others' encouragement I attempted this, but I soon found it was not something I could initiate at will. Many of the mature trees, like the one in which I spent the storm and this Gnome Oak (whose burl I've been resting on this past while) have remained inexplicably closed to me. Still, I did have a few successes. While none of them approached the profound rapport I had experienced with the ancient pine above the river, one was every bit as instructive: an exchange with the Conference Oak in front of the farmhouse, the very tree I sat beneath that day I first shared my plan to save the forest.

This nearly three-hundred-year-old white oak did not, of course, communicate verbally. Yet it radiated its knowing with a power and a clarity that proved quite effective in conveying its understanding. It taught me a great deal about its nature and about the nature of trees in general. It helped me see that, among other things, my long-standing policy of never cutting down a living tree was preventing me from providing the forest with the kind of care it needed— and needed badly.

Since the Conference Oak's communication was nonverbal, I can only paraphrase it here.

"You must understand," the old oak explained, "there are two types of tree consciousness: collective and individual. Collective tree consciousness contains individual tree beings, like myself, who have roots in generalized tree consciousness, just as we have roots in the earth. When a sapling rises from the forest soil, it is an expression of our generalized consciousness, with little or no individuality.

"Not until a tree has matured does it possess sufficient circuitry to accommodate an individual tree spirit. Even then, amid the physical and psychic crowding of so many saplings, few trees in these forests today mature sufficiently to attract the grand—you might say, archangelic—presences that graced the American forests in ancient times. This is why we appreciate, and in fact require, thinning.

"Without conscientious thinning of this forest by those who understand these things, it would—assuming we were left on our own—take us close to a thousand years to reestablish ourselves in forms that would allow this forest to achieve full awareness. With conscientious thinning, we could reach that state in just over a century. But what is far more important, with proper management we could, in just two or three centuries, bring into certain of our mature forms a level of cooperative intelligence beyond any previously embodied in this planet's trees. This would have great advantages for humans as well as for us. It would benefit other forest creatures and the earth as a whole."

TAKING MY LEAVE OF THE GNOME OAK and its hive of honey bees, I see the First Rocks' pool through a tangle of multiflora rose bushes on my right. A shaft of afternoon sunlight has found its way through the trees to the west to illuminate the rock island in the center of the pool like a stage. Enjoying the spotlight, a bright yellow finch preens himself in the reflecting surface of the water, while nearby, a pair of iridescent-blue buntings cautiously work their way down the branches of a dogwood toward the warm shallows just south of the sunlit island.

At the pool's headwaters I settle cross-legged behind an arrowwood bush. Each of what I first take for individual arrowwood flowers proves on closer inspection to be domed clusters, packed with dozens of separate flowers—white, with yellow cores, each centered by a tiny pupil of white. The blossoms reach upward, seeming to welcome the ants, bees, and green-and-black ladybugs that are taking quite an interest in them.

While a cardinal and a rose-breasted grosbeak watch from a branch overhead, a bright orange bird—a scarlet tanager, a male by his coloring—bathes not three feet from me in the pond. Ignoring my presence, he dunks his head, flaps his black-streaked wings, and splashes water contentedly round about. Like the other birds, he seems to prefer

bathing in this shallow basin where the water is undoubtedly warmer than in the deeper areas around it.

Plump and full, as are most birds at this time of
year, a young robin flies down and lands at his side.
She looks like the same robin who was making such a
commotion earlier this morning. While both she and
the tanager remain bathing, a blue jay flies down to
join them.

To see these three brightly colored birds—one red,
one bright blue, and the third orange and black—all
in the same little pool at the same time is a rare sight.
Suddenly their three disparate voices flower into si-
multaneous song. They're jamming! Whether the result is a symphony or a cacophony depends on your
point of view, but I do think their session would
sound better without the jay.

Apparently the robin shares my opinion. She
pauses thoughtfully in her song, hops over to the jay's
side, and, with what appears to be a mumbled comment, begins bathing wildly, splashing water in his direction and giving him quite a soaking. When this has
no effect, she lunges at the bright blue bird, chasing
the would-be songster away. This does not surprise
me. Besides being poor vocalists, jays often eat blue-
bird and robin eggs, and few of us, when you stop to
consider it, would be comfortable caroling with someone who would breakfast on our children.

People living in the Ozarks today don't have to
worry about predators, but this wasn't always the
case. There was a time when the people who drew
their water from our spring shared this very hollow
with saber-toothed tigers, giant ground sloths, lions,
panthers, mastodons. They knew winters when
wolves literally appeared at their doors. These days
when the wolf is at the door, people whimper and call

for more government spending. But those ancient Ozarkers? Archaeological evidence indicates that when the wolf showed up at their door, they barbecued it and tanned its hide.

This has never been a rich or fertile land, yet it compensates by drawing out the resourcefulness of those who are determined to make it their home. Humans have lived here for well over ten thousand years, and the same practicality that characterized our predecessors is found in those who live here today.

When hard times hit, the rest of the nation must learn how to adapt. Ozarkers are already used to them. Since the first settlers of European descent arrived here in the middle of the last century, our economy has been in a sort of perpetual recession. But just as Aesop's turtle wound up winning his race with the hare, we are the better for it, I believe. For despite its own share of consumer excess, our Ozark economy is rooted in the land—a reality that will endure long after those flashy economies whose survival depends on a daily fix of fossil fuels have faded into the footnotes of history.

If you are willing to forgo some of the frills of the mainstream consumer economy in exchange for clear air, rugged land, and a healthy moral climate, these mountains will meet you halfway and show you new and often surprising ways of securing the *true* necessities.

Only twice in twenty years here have I been unemployed, and only a few days each time. On the first of these occasions, after exhausting ordinary channels of application, I went house to house looking for work. Beginning one morning on Highway 17 north of Summersville, I started with the houses on the west side of the highway, planning to turn around if I had not found work by noon and make my way homeward while applying at houses on the highway's east side.

"I'm willing to work for minimum wage," I'd explain when the door was answered. "I can do about anything you want done by way of carpentry, plumbing, masonry, trees cut, fences mended, roofs repaired, odd jobs. If a dollar eighty-five an hour is too much for you, we can talk about it, maybe work it out in trade or something. I've got tools and equipment in my truck and can start now if you've got something needs doing."

Dale Brashers answered the third door I knocked upon and hired me on for the next six months. Of all the jobs I have ever held, this one made the deepest and most lasting impression on my children.

At the time he hired me, Dale had leased for use in his well-drilling business a brand-new, state-of-the-art Bucyrus-Erie high-pressured, rotary well-drilling rig. It was an awesome piece of machinery, as loud as a 747 revving up for takeoff, and sometimes audible up to twenty miles away. Everywhere within a five-hundred-yard radius of its operation the ground trembled like the San Andreas fault during a latitude adjustment.

Although I wore double ear plugs—both the foam type that you roll up and stick in your ears and the headphone type that you wear over them like ear muffs—my whole body would vibrate so much from all the pounding and shaking that I literally heard through my bones. The rig's operation so impressed my children that when they first viewed it from our pickup truck, it took Sherry fifteen minutes to pry Becky's hands off the steering wheel and coax baby Fin out from behind the front seat. What made this job their all-time favorite, though, was the way I looked when I came home from work.

Each time we drove another twenty-foot section of the six-inch drill bit its full length into the earth, we had to back off and raise it a few inches before unscrewing it from the rig to attach another twenty-foot section. Whenever we did this, the sudden release of compressed air and water would splatter everything in range with a sloppy wet muck—the most god-awful blast of slime that any child ever hoped to see. It was wonderful . . . that is, in a sick sort of way that's difficult to explain to anyone who isn't a well driller, or possibly a Mets fan.

We would try not to get sprayed, of course, but it did little good. We were spitting mud out of our teeth half the time and wiping it from our eyes the rest. By the time I returned home from work in the evenings, my hands, face, and coveralls would be caked and dripping with mud. Only a pair of familiar eyes told the children that it was me and not some terrible monster from the depths staggering up the path to their door. The job made such an impression on them that I have detected their disappointment in every job I've taken since.

The only other time I was unemployed, our situation was more serious. During winter, carpentry jobs are scarce even in a good year, but this particular winter there were none whatsoever. We were nearly out of money, and what was far more troubling, we would soon be out of the grain we needed to feed our milk cow. Our supplies of kerosene, oatmeal, shortening, rice, and other store-bought necessities were running dangerously low; and even finding enough gas money to go out and look for work was becoming difficult.

If we hadn't already fallen in love with Shannon County, I'm sure we would have that winter when a social worker from our county welfare office took the time to make a thirty-mile trip to our house, attempting to get us to sign up for welfare. It was a caring gesture, but we declined. We were still eating well, none of us was in danger of malnutrition, and I was determined to exhaust every employment possibility before hollering 'nuff and accepting a government handout.

Since knocking on doors had worked once, it might, I reasoned, work again. So with tools loaded in the back of my truck, I headed down the dirt road, intending this time to look for potential employers among those who lived on the east side of Highway 17.

On the way I pulled into the Y Grocery for gas. I was standing at the pump, my tank half full, when Granny, the proprietress, stuck her head out the door.

"Kenny," she said, "one of your relatives called. Left his number. You're supposed to call."

No credit card number in those phoneless days, so I got myself a fist full of quarters, pumped a half dozen of them into the antique on the wall, and rang up the number, hoping that no one had died. It took a while for a series of operators to extract my call from the primitive tangle of party lines that to this day still plagues many rural parts of the Ozarks, but the call was finally put through, and my brother-in-law, Louie, answered.

Louie, who had married Sherry's sister Linda, was a garbage collector in Darien, Connecticut, one of New York City's wealthiest suburbs. His route wove through a fairytale setting of exquisite multimillion-dollar homes resting among magnificent, three-hundred-year-old trees. Keeping up with the Joneses here meant more than just removing dandelions from your

lawn. It meant hiring professional landscapers to im-
peccably manicure your own private botanical gardens.

"There's been a real bad ice storm," Louie said.
"Trees down all over the place. There's not enough
guys with chain saws around here to clean them up
fast enough for these people, who are all wanting it
done yesterday. A friend of mine, Andy, has a crew
going around cleaning things up. He says he's got
four or five times more work than he can handle. Said
he could really use you and your chain saw. He'll pay
you four dollars an hour plus cover the cost of your
travel out here. You're welcome to stay here with me
and Linda. Can you hop on the bus?"

Well, there it was. I had a job.

The next day Sherry drove me to the liquor store in
Willow Springs that doubles as our local bus stop, and
almost before I knew it I was on my way to that place
I had so far succeeded in avoiding—New York City.

Watching the afternoon sunlight filter through the
white oak leaves above, and the birds bathing before
me in the pool, it is hard to believe in New York.

Does the same sun that plays with the shadows of
leaves and wildflowers on this forest floor really shine
simultaneously—this very moment—on mile-high
towers of glass and steel? It is difficult to comprehend
how the same planet could accommodate two so very
different places. But Yeats made it work, writing
"Lake Isle of Innisfree"—indeed, his best pastoral
verse—while holed up in the thick of London. Surely,
I thought, I could handle a week or two in the
shadow of Manhattan.

Transferring in St. Louis to the bus that would
take me to New York, I had made a point to be at the

head of the line in order to claim the backseat, so if the bus didn't fill up I'd have room to stretch out and catch some sleep during the twenty-four-hour drive. When the bus pulled out of St. Louis only a fraction full, I was comfortably ensconced in its rear. But I was restless and more than a little concerned about my family. I wanted nothing more than to reach my destination, sharpen up my Stihl—041 AV electronic ignition top-of-the-line—chain saw, and get right to work.

There had been no chance to sharpen the saw before I left home. By the time I had pumped enough change into the pay phone to line things up with Andy, I had only enough time to remove its bar and chain and pack the parts in a pair of duffel bags alongside my clothes.

I watched the Illinois landscape roll past with some interest, since it was the state where I had grown up, but not long into the utter monotony of central Indiana I grew bored and restless. The Louis L'Amour novel I had hoped would occupy me during the long ride had barely lasted the two-hour stopover in St. Louis, and I longed to be working, doing something.

Might as well sharpen my chain saw, I thought, one less thing I'll have to do when I arrive. With an hour or so of remaining daylight I'd have plenty of time to do a first-class job.

Now, in order to sharpen a chain saw, the chain has got to be on the saw. You can't just hold it loose in your hand like a piece of spaghetti and successfully file its teeth. Opening up my shirt duffel bag, I removed the bright red Stihl 041 AV engine. From my pants duffel bag I withdrew the bar and chain and the two nuts that held it on. It took only a minute to put it all together, adjust the tension on the chain, and tighten down the nuts—I had done it many times before.

From a shirt pocket I extracted my Carlton file-o-plate, and with a sense of pleasure, feeling the familiar about me again, I slowly began putting a razor edge on each of the twenty-one-inch chain's thirty-six teeth.

Sitting in the middle of the Greyhound's backseat, and supporting the bar of the chain saw on an arm of the empty seat in front, gave my elbow plenty of clearance as I worked the file back and forth. I had filed all the left-facing teeth and had started on the right before I began to feel that sense of unease that signals to us mammals that something is wrong, dreadfully wrong.

I looked up.

Everyone had moved to the front of the bus—right close to the driver, whose face I could see glancing up at me nervously in the rearview mirror as he mumbled something into a CB microphone. With a shock I realized that these people were afraid.

Afraid of me? My mind would not accept it at first—it was so out of step with my self-image. My children loved me. Folks I worked with seemed to think I was OK. I caught a glimpse of myself in the window: bushy black beard, worn denim jacket, hair tied back in a ponytail. And we were, after all, passing through the conservative heartland at a time when most men—*I'll be damned. There's an Indiana state trooper driving alongside the bus, and there's another one behind us, lights flashing!* The bus pulled over and stopped beneath an overpass.

State troopers were everywhere.

What followed was anticlimactic. A couple of teenaged passengers and one of the younger officers even looked a bit disappointed as I explained what I

had been doing and why. They asked me to keep the
chain saw stashed until I got to New York. I agreed,
and that was that. But it was a somewhat sobered
Ken who gazed thoughtfully out the window as the
bus sped on through the deepening twilight of that
lonely winter landscape. My lack of sensitivity troubled me. I had experienced my own share of run-ins
with people whose behavior was as myopic as mine
had been, people so caught up in themselves that
they failed to notice when their actions intruded
upon others; and I didn't like to think of myself in
that category. I resolved that in the future I would
try to be more aware of those around me. It wasn't
until I returned home and mentioned it to Sherry
that it occurred to me to look at it in a humorous
light.

A light breeze ripples the leaves of the arrowwood
as I turn to find the source of a scuffling sound behind me. Tentatively, a chipper young squirrel spirals
down the trunk of a nearby hickory, studies me a moment, and, deciding I am harmless, scampers over to
the pool's edge for a drink. Even as I watch him, my
thoughts linger on that winter's journey. Perhaps it
stands out in my memory because back then it was
one of the few opportunities I had for contemplation.

As the bus passed through the Amish country of
Pennsylvania, I thought of the smaller Amish community with which I was associated back in Missouri.
Since they used only horses and buggies for trans-
portation—and would not otherwise have been able
to make the two-hundred-mile round trip in less than
several days—I would often drive them to Sunday
meetings in the Seymour area where there is a much

larger Amish community. The image it first presented to me is one I will never forget. As my truck cleared the crest of a small hill, I found myself looking out across a landscape I had thought long vanished from the American scene.

Before me stretched a green valley isolated by a ring of thickly wooded hills. In its center stood an old but freshly painted farmhouse, white, with green shutters. Beyond it was a barn of Pennsylvania Dutch design and a windmill slowly turning in the morning breeze.

Beneath the shade of the mature oaks and elms surrounding the house and barn stood nearly thirty horse-drawn carriages. No power lines. No motorized vehicles. Just a pristine rural landscape that looked as though it could have been the inspiration for a nineteenth-century Currier and Ives.

For a fleeting instant I wished that this glimpse of a preindustrial way of life might signal the end of my own search for "the right way" to pass my time upon this earth. Yet I knew it could never be. I am simultaneously cursed and blessed with too inquisitive a mind ever to settle into any religion's prescribed system of thought. As for promised eternal rewards, I was never one to hold my breath.

Whether despite or because of their doctrinal hardheadedness, my Amish neighbors had achieved some very real successes. Their farms were picture perfect; their family ties, strong; their children, cheerful and surprisingly mischievous. As an apprentice to an Amish carpenter, I worked with them on a daily basis. When someone needed a house built or a barn raised, everyone turned out. We once built a house in a single day. Of all their achievements, it was this sense of community that most impressed me.

While I was inclined to dismiss many of their "evils" as mere overreactions to the militarism rejected by their seventeenth-century founder, I had to admit that the moral code of which they were a part had, at least in Mountain View, produced a spiritually as well as a materially healthy community.

Like many native American traditions, Amish customs take into account the well-being of generations beyond their own. I disagreed—in some instances vehemently—with many of their taboos. Yet on a smoky Greyhound en route to Manhattan with my chain saw, I knew that I was in no position to say that one way of life was right and the other wrong.

As time passed I often wished that I had written some account of these thoughts that mingled with the steady drone of the bus as it sped through the night, for all too soon I had forgotten them, caught up again in the world's penny-wise, pound-foolish pragmatism. I made good money in Connecticut. The work was steady and I was able to put in long hours each day. But I soon learned that while I and the others were earning four dollars an hour, our boss, Andy, was charging customers twelve dollars an hour for each of us and pocketing the difference—a custom unheard-of in the Ozarks. Incredulous, that night over supper I informed Louie of my discovery.

"Common practice here," he said. "Just about everyone does it."

Then and there I decided to keep my eyes open for some freelance work. Louie's collection route took him through the very center of the wealthy community where I worked with Andy and his crew. Maybe he could help me bypass the middleman.

Between servings of lasagna and garlic bread, I suggested the idea, and thanks to a long-standing tradition among the Biancos, Louie's family, I presented my case with eloquence. With their evening meal that night they served some of their homemade wine, made from specially grown old-world grapes fermented in fifty-five-gallon barrels of seasoned oak according to an ancient family recipe dating back to the vineyards of Tuscany. As the meal progressed I felt increasingly at home amid the warmth and closeness of Louie's parents, brothers, and sisters. Mr. Bianco himself broke open a cask of their best and poured each of us a generous measure of the clear white wine, ceremoniously handing me, the honored guest, the first measure.

It had been several years since I had consumed any alcoholic beverage, and even then it had been only an occasional beer. To avoid being rude, I raised a glass of the clear fluid, which resembled nothing so much as water, and took a few polite sips. I was amazed. The taste was of open fields, sunshine, and fresh summer rain. Deceived by what I mistakenly took for its low alcohol content, before I knew it my glass was empty and in the process of being refilled.

"So you like it, son?" Mr. Bianco asked. I waxed eloquent. My relief at being able to drink with the others was enhanced by sincere enthusiasm for the quality of their wine.

"Louie," I said expansively, "you come from a big family. I come from a big family. We don't have time for in-laws—you and me—we're brothers."

"Spoken like a true Italian," said Linda, laughing.

There was a toast. The whole family joined in, even the younger children. Louie's father was visibly moved and insisted on refilling my cup yet again. Amid this conducive atmosphere, Louie and I laid our plans, and he agreed to help me line up some independent work.

By the following evening he was able to tell me of a lawyer who had a tree in his backyard that had died a few summers ago. The lawyer, Louie said, wanted it removed before it fell on his house or the nearby barn, which his wife had renovated as her art studio. He had taken bids, Louie explained, from local landscaping services, but they were all in the thousand-dollar-and-up range.

"For cutting down one tree?"

"I looked at it on my route today," Louie explained. "It sets like this . . . " He pulled out a napkin and proceeded to draw a diagram. An X represented the tree, a little square, the house, and a pair of parallel lines, the driveway. A square showed the barn that now served as art studio. Then he inked in the shed and the power lines, which passed within twenty feet of the tree, and, last, drew a shaded rectangle showing the location of the arboretum. He concluded with several emphatic circles around the X that marked the tree's location, explaining that it was an old elm, about seventy feet tall and nearly three feet in diameter.

"There's only one spot," he pointed out, "where you can drop it without damaging something. Right here, parallel with the power lines, just missing the edge of the house, falling away from the driveway and kind of catywampus from the art studio."

"Won't it clip the arboretum if it falls like that?" Linda asked, looking over our shoulders at the diagram.

"I don't think so, not if he gets it in there just right. But I'm no expert. Ken, why don't you come along with me on my route tomorrow and see what you think. The reason the landscapers quoted such high bids is because their insurance companies won't let them just go in there and cut it down straightforward-like. To satisfy their insurance people, they've got to follow stringent guidelines that require them to bring in a cherry picker, start at the top, and remove the branches one at a time, lowering each one with a cable to the ground until what's left of the trunk is small enough to fall the direction they want without taking any risks. Doing it that way calls for heavy equipment and a crew of four or five guys. And it would probably take them the better part of an afternoon."

"You know, I may be wrong here, Louie, but it seems to me someone who knew what they were doing could set that sucker right where they wanted it, first time, no problem. I can generally make a tree fall anywhere I want. Just notch 'er in the direction you want 'er to fall, rise up a bit and cut in from the backside about halfway through, then—to be on the safe side—do the rest with wedges and a sledge. I brought my steel wedges, but I'll probably make up a few wooden ones for a job like this, so if the saw chain accidentally nicks one it won't chip a tooth. That way I'll be able to cut deeper here and there with the saw even after the wedges are in place."

"That's all there is to it?"

"No, you've got to watch the top of the tree as you're doing the final cutting. If you keep your eye on it while you're making that final cut—real slow and easy-like, just cutting through a fraction of an inch at a time—you can see right off if the tree starts to lean even slightly in the wrong direction."

"What do you do if it does?"

"Well, if I start to see it heading the wrong way, I shut off the saw and do the rest with the wedges and sledgehammer, guiding it pretty much wherever I want it to go. If you don't mind, I'll borrow that six-teen-pound mallet I saw in your garage."

"Sounds like you've done this before."

"A fair amount. Most of the time," I admitted, "I don't bother with wedges. Usually don't need them if you do it right. They're just for insurance really, but probably worth using in a situation like this."

"Your trees always fall the way you want them to?"

"All but once," I said, remembering when a sixty-foot black oak, despite everything I had done, fell backward on my wedges. Luckily it didn't do much damage, just pushed down a barbed wire fence and popped out a few staples—didn't even break the wire. Even so, it was embarrassing. As I told about it, Linda pointed out that it would be a little more than embarrassing if the tree in question fell anywhere but that one open spot.

"If it hits these power lines here," Louie said, gesturing on the napkin, "it'll likely knock out power for the whole southeast corner of Darien; at the very least all the homes in that area would be out for the rest of the day. Somebody'd get sued for sure. Every other door you knock on along there belongs to a lawyer, or someone who retains a half dozen of them. Most of them wouldn't think anything of tossing out a lawsuit after you. You sure you want to risk it?"

"Tell you what, Louie. These are your customers, people you've known for years, and you've got to live with them, so I won't approach it this way if you don't want me to, but if you have no objections, I'll just load up my Stihl, your splitting mall, the wedges, and a few other odds and ends, and go ask 'Leeny (Sherry and Linda's youngest sister) to drive me out there first thing in the morning. I'll take a look at the tree. If it looks like I can drop it all right, I'll put in a bid and go for it right there on the spot, if they're agreeable."

"Couldn't be more than a few hours' work doing it that way. You got any idea what you're gonna bid?"

"Well," I said, feeling a little guilty for asking so much, "I was thinking of asking somewhere around a hundred dollars. Do you think that'd be fair?"

"A hundred dollars! Tell him you'll do it for a hundred dollars and he'll jump at it! Him and his wife are wanting that tree down real bad. They just can't see paying a thousand bucks."

"So my plan's OK?"

Louie grinned. "So long as you don't screw it up."

Early the next morning I loaded up the chain saw, gas, oil, sixteen-pound sledgehammer, and Louie's splitting mall, which I had sharpened the night before since splitting and stacking the wood would likely be expected.

I realized, of course, that my approach to this enterprise had left certain ethical questions somewhat less than thoroughly explored, and I will not now, in retrospect, pretend that what I did was exemplary. It wasn't. But this was one of those murky areas where the line between right and wrong seemed broad enough for a zoning ordinance, and my action cannot be judged without taking into account the context in which it occurred. It took me twenty-five hours—over three full days—to earn $100 working for Andy, and by the time he had taken out social security and taxes, it was whittled down to a mere $73.50.

If I could pull this off, I'd be earning the better part of a week's wages in a couple of hours. I knew how far that money would go back in the Ozarks, the food it would put on our shelves, and how happy it would make Sherry and the kids. Besides, I was in a sweat to get home, and this would give me the option of returning earlier than planned.

So it didn't seem too terribly wrong at the time to explain to Eileen as she turned into the long drive that approached the house, "Listen, 'Leeny, you just sit out here in the car with the engine running. There's only a small chance that anything will go wrong, but in the unlikely event it does, I'll, uh, be needing some breathing space while I consider my options. You'll know in a minute or so how things went.

"Either I'll come walking around the side of the house with a grin on my face, giving you the thumbs-up signal—in which case you can go do your errands and come back and pick me up in a couple of hours after I've split the wood—or . . . I'll come tearing around the side of the house in a god-awful hurry. If I do, just push open this door and as soon as I'm in, shove that pedal to the floor and we're out of here. But, really, don't look so worried. I expect that tree's going to drop just where I aim to."

And it did. It was that simple. Within five minutes I had that old elm laid out just where I wanted it. The next couple of hours were the real work, sawing and splitting the mammoth old tree into firewood, but I worked with a song in my heart, too busy to ponder what might have been.

THE GREEKS HAVE A SINGLE WORD that means both "crowning virtue" and "tragic flaw." Its American translation could well be "Ozark," for when all is said and done, the greatest wealth of these hills is their very poverty.

With no great rivers for access, and no more than a few inches of topsoil, the Ozarks are unsuited to both manufacturing and agribusiness on any significant scale. What soil we do have is scattered across rocky ground so rugged that often an acre as legally measured will contain two or three acres of wrinkled hollows and jagged hillsides. Or as I once heard an old-timer in Eminence put it, "If you was to take Shannon County up north a ways, peg down an edge and stretch out her wrinkles, why ah reckon she'd cover the better part of Iowa."

Those who visit here from other parts of the world are often amazed to hear the ages of our trees. An Ozark oak no more than ten inches in diameter can be as much as a half century old. Ultimately the poor soil works to a tree's advantage. When it grows slowly, its rings are closer together, its wood is denser, and it is better able to withstand a storm.

Just south of the First Rocks pond here is a hickory that never seems to grow at all. When I first saw it nearly two decades ago, I doubted that it would survive another season, for it's performing a task more in the province of Houdini than of botany.

The hickory has but a single root; and before this lone root turns upward to become the main trunk, it actually leaves the ground and traverses a foot of empty space! This gives the impression that the total weight of the tree is resting on nothing but a sort of open-air amphitheater. Adding further peril to this uncertain footing, its trunk, when finally deciding to head upward, does so without much enthusiasm, leaning languidly above the rocks at an angle perhaps thirty degrees shy of perpendicular. But what amazes me most about this tree, like so many others in this area, is not this apparent defiance of gravity, but the fact that year after year it always looks the same. Twenty years ago its diameter was about eight inches, and so it remains.

Today these Shannon County mountains are covered with hardwood forests; and throughout the Ozarks, where forests still exist, they, too, are predominantly hardwoods. They seem to suit the region so well that I had lived here several years assuming this had always been the case. I discovered my error while hiking through the woods one morning with the local surveyor. It was during the early months of the Greenwood Forest Project, and we were marking off the southern boundary of the land whose trees we hoped to protect. For reference we had brought along the maps and written records of previous surveyors.

As we stood atop a ridge overlooking the Jacks Fork River, it was both disturbing and thought-provoking to hear read aloud the notes of the first man to have surveyed this area, back in 1841: "As far as I can see," he wrote, "the hills are covered with towering virgin pine."

We were standing in the exact spot where he had written those words, and from our vantage point we could see several square miles of forest. Few of the trees we saw were pine. One does see an occasional stand here and there, more easily spotted in the winter when the deciduous trees have dropped their leaves, but who would have thought that as recently as 1841 Ozark forests could have been so different? Many of those trees grew to twice the height of the tallest trees here today, and it is said that some were so large that an entire house could be built from their lumber.

In many ways I am proud of our American culture. Our Yankee ingenuity has blessed the world with unparalleled medical, technological, and scientific advances. Yet hearing the words of that nineteenth-century surveyor, I only wanted to hang my head in shame. It isn't that I necessarily think the lumber was wasted; but the trees are gone now—and where is the wood? In all but a few cases, it has long since rotted away. Was it used, I wonder, to build St. Louis? Little Rock? Kansas City? No doubt it formed many of the false storefronts in the western towns that sprouted and then so quickly faded from the plains.

These towns, these cities, their industries, their needs—were they worth the destruction of thirty thousand square miles of ancient trees?

A friend of mine claims that the true measure of a community is whether the trees are numbered in the census along with the people. I have to agree—at least if it is to be a community that would interest me.

The first community in which I can remember walking down the street and playing outdoors was a west-side Chicago neighborhood where my parents

had rented a flat in a yellow-brick apartment building. Later we moved to our own house, but it was
sandwiched so tightly among so many others that
even from the dizzying three-hundred-foot height of
our local water tower I could see no more than the
hazy skyline and buildings stretching off in every direction. I could not understand why people wanted to
live in such crowded conditions, let alone mortgage
thirty years of their lives for the privilege.

By the time my still-partying high school friends
had staggered out of their liberal arts colleges and
sobered up to the fact that their student loans actually had to be repaid, I had bought and paid for my
first home, was completely out of debt, and had
banked two thousand dollars to help us get started on
these eighty rural acres.

True, our home rested on a foundation of six large
rocks and was basically just a five-hundred-square-
foot shanty with so many chinks and openings in its
uninsulated walls that—even with doors and win-
dows shut—the wind on a stormy night would sometimes extinguish the kerosene lamp on our kitchen
table. But there is something to be said for owning a
place outright.

A full basement, mortgaged, is not half so solid
a foundation as six bought-and-paid-for rocks. We
were, as they say, "beholden to none." Good footings
for a couple of kids in their early twenties, a solid
foundation upon which Sherry and I could—and
did—build the rest of our lives.

And we had no shortage of help in getting started.

The first of our neighbors to visit us here were
Frank and Clyde Lynch. The day we met them our
noon meal was interrupted by a general exodus into
the yard to identify a rattling sound that was slowly

approaching from the north. By the time they pulled up outside the house and brought their truck to a stop, we were already out there to greet them.

Clyde, a woman in her early sixties, wasted no time in telling us that she had grown up in the house in which we were living. That didn't surprise me. The place looked like it could have been Noah's boyhood home. What surprised me was her comment that our house still had the same tin roof on it that it did when she was a girl! That roof, she said, had been on there since before she was born! How long before, she wasn't sure. The tin was a dull, rusty red when we moved in, but by the time of this visit, I had renailed it, caulked the seams, and applied several coats of silver-colored roof cement.

"Last you another hundred years if you take care of it like that," Frank said.

The Lynches were impressed with the small things we had done and took an immediate liking to us, which we found easy to reciprocate. Later I learned that we were the only young people they knew at that time who were raising a family much as they had been raised—without electricity or plumbing, hauling our water from a nearby spring, growing most of our own food, cooking on a wood cook stove, and so on.

Frank told us he used to live just a mile or so away in a little cabin back by Gilmore Pond, a cabin that was still standing then, though it is now long gone.

"Be back there still if it weren't for her," he said, nodding to Clyde. "She don't like to be back in that fur. Wants to be out there along the road where she can see the folks goin' by." Then, pausing to look around approvingly, "I'd a bought this place if it was upta me. You got a good spot here."

We agreed.

After the Lynches had shown us features of the land that we had overlooked—including a spot where an orchard had once stood and where a few plum trees remained—Frank went back for his near-prehistoric tractor and proceeded to plow our garden free of charge. Being in his seventies didn't slow him down. He was out there in the woods several days a week cutting fence posts in exchange for what few necessities he and Clyde no longer produced for themselves.

As the months passed, other neighbors stopped by. Charles Harsh showed us wild edibles growing in our woods and pasture, and his wife, Jessie, taught us how to prepare them. When my truck lost all interest in mobility—as it generally did a month or two each year—Cletus Hendricks would meet me at the mailbox and let me ride into work with him. When my pickup truck did run, but only long enough to settle up to its axles in mud, Will McVicker or Olive Hines would drive a tractor over and pull me out, becoming insulted if I offered to pay them for their trouble. And throughout the long years when our family's annual income was less than twenty-five hundred dollars, local businesses extended me credit, without once asking me to fill out a credit application.

When push finally came to shove and I reluctantly went to the Bank of Mountain View requesting a five-thousand-dollar loan, its manager, Henry Justis, didn't seem to be paying much attention. He quickly changed the subject to beekeeping, a topic of mutual interest as we both kept hives in conjunction with our orchards. His casual friendliness was all well and good, but after a half-hour discussion of extraction techniques, replacement of queens, and methods of dealing with foul brood, I gently guided the discussion back to the purpose of my visit.

"Oh, that," Henry replied, losing interest. "My secretary's got the papers all filled out." (He had handed her a note shortly after I arrived.) "You can go sign them anytime. Money's already in your account. But about these African bees now, I think the media has blown the whole thing out of proportion; the way I look at it . . . "

So I came home to the Ozarks.

But of all our neighbors, Frank and Clyde Lynch were the most helpful. Sipping coffee around the fire in our potbellied stove and listening to their stories about the century's early decades, we felt we were very nearly back there. Highway 17 was a dirt road, and Bunker Hill Road, not much more than a glorified deer trail. There was no bridge across the Jacks Fork River, so twice a month on Saturdays they would hitch up their horses and wagon and ford the river to get into town for supplies. It was a time when cars were almost unheard-of in this area.

"Even if folks could afford them," Clyde explained, "and most couldn't, the dirt roads were so rough they'd tear 'em up in no time. They just weren't worth foolin' with."

"It'd take most of a morning to get into town," Frank went on. "We'd ford the river down there where the 17 bridge is now, not gettin' into Mountain View till nearly noon. We'd do our shoppin' and hope to get home before dark, but we hardly ever made it. Didn't matter much though. Comin' home I'd just throw down the reins and fall asleep—couldn't see anything most a the time anyway. Those horses knew where to go. They'd take us right to our front door."

I asked Clyde if during her time growing up in the farmhouse, her family had depended, as we did, on the cistern for their washing water. "What cistern?" she asked. I showed her. Opening the lid that covered the fourteen-foot-deep, six-foot-diameter hole under the back porch, I explained to her and Frank how I had installed gutters to channel in the rainwater, and how—to keep out groundwater contaminants—I had just finished coating its walls with three coats of waterproof cement.

"So, you plastered up the well," Frank said dryly.

"Well?" I asked in surprise. "I thought it was a cistern."

"It *was* a well. Used to be a good one, too. Don't worry though. Your plaster'll all be washed out in a month or so."

Sure enough. After a few rains, water seepage had pushed it all in. Apparently that groundwater seepage had been enough to provide Clyde and her family with their basic needs, but I can't help thinking they must have played it mighty close at times.

While my plaster job proved unnecessary, the gutter hookup did keep the cistern filled to the brim with charcoal filtered rainwater, which—since we hauled our drinking water from the spring—we used primarily for washing. Our problem was that while the cistern provided adequate water for our washing needs, and the spring for our cooking and drinking, neither provided a surplus. And both were dependent on rain, which just didn't come often enough during summer months for even a hope of watering our garden. When it doesn't rain for six or seven weeks and you've got an acre or more under cultivation (and fifty or sixty young fruit trees) this can be serious.

"You ever want to put you in a deep well," Frank said one day, "you let me know. I'll witch it for you."

"You a water witcher?"

"Best one hereabouts," Clyde said. "He'll witch you a spot where you'll get plenty a water."

"Won't be anytime soon," I explained, "much as they cost. But whenever we're ready to drill, Frank, you can be sure we'll have you witch it for us."

Now, while our neighbor was the *local* water witcher—and by all accounts the best in the region—as the years passed and I worked in the area between Mountain View and West Plains (a dozen miles beyond a river that in the old days was more like a state line), I heard a great deal of talk about some water witcher named Charlie. Whenever the subject came up, it was always Charlie-this and Charlie-that.

It soon became clear that this Charlie character was virtually famous for his dowsing and was considered by many to be the finest water witcher in the central Ozarks. But the fact never impressed me much. Charlie hailed from a highway town, and I could see how a witcher might grow famous there, while a better one could pass unnoticed in our unsettled corner of the woods. Frank was a modest man, uninterested, it seemed to me, in such superficialities. Since I had already promised him the job, I paid little attention to all the Charlie stories floating about.

After the terrible drought of 1977, when keeping our summer garden from turning tarmac required hand pumping our cistern dry two or three times a week (and hiring a truck to refill it each time), we decided to put in a well. Other summers had been nearly as dry and it was just too painful to watch the vegetables that we counted on for the better part of our diet wither away.

We sold our Ford 2000 diesel tractor for thirty-five hundred dollars—more than a year's wages in those simpler times—and we sank every penny of the proceeds into a hole in the ground small enough to cover with a dinner plate. A hole in the ground that was useless without a pump, a gasoline engine, and nearly four hundred feet of sucker rod and costly two-inch pipe. For months we tried to save for these, but it seemed that every time we got a dollar or two put aside, our truck would find out about it and have a breakdown calculated to match our savings.

We could see only one way to get the water flowing from our well in time for the garden. We sold our pickup truck and bought what we needed. This left me to commute to work on a ten-speed bicycle—a twenty-eight-mile round trip up and down hills so steep I had to walk in places, but it was worth it. When finally in operation, our well proved itself one of the most dependable in the area, and we had Frank to thank for it. We drilled right where he said we would find our most reliable source of water—and we did. But the circumstances surrounding Frank's choice of that well site, and the way he went about dowsing it, demolished every image I'd ever had about water witching.

Things would undoubtedly have gone better if I'd had greater faith in the dowser's art, but the truth is, by the time we were ready to drill our well, I had completely forgotten about water witching. By then I had worked half a year with Dale Brashers, one of the best well drillers in the region. From firsthand experience I had learned that if you wanted a dependable water source, you needed to get down into the water table.

While the depth of the water table does indeed vary slightly with fluctuations of the surface terrain, in our area it usually runs three hundred to four hundred feet below the surface, with very little variation. (The fact is, at that depth the water is there. You can drill anywhere and get into it as long as you drill deep enough.)

This is not to say that water witchers—especially in the old days—did not perform a valuable service. A good witcher can supposedly detect the course of underground streams that are often much closer to the surface than the water table. When wells were dug by hand or horse power, knowing the location of such streams could save months of backbreaking work. However, these underground streams usually stop flowing during dry spells, precisely when our garden would most need watering. Since we wanted the dependability of a deep well, as the time neared to drill one, water witchers were the furthest thing from my mind.

For months we had been discussing with friends and neighbors our plans to drill a well, so I shouldn't have been surprised to see our friends Doug and Wilma show up on the construction site one afternoon with old Charlie himself. As the three of them converged on the spot where I was working, it was obvious what they had on their minds. Doug had been telling me about Charlie for months, and not wanting to be rude (a weakness everyone assures me I have since overcome) I must have inadvertently given the impression that when the time came I would ask Charlie to dowse the location for us.

The old man said not a word as Doug and Wilma told me the good news: Charlie was free at the moment, and since I was about to get off work . . . Well, Doug did a bit of arm-twisting, and unable to think of a graceful way to turn Charlie down to his face, the next thing I knew everyone had agreed to follow me home so this reputed water witcher could dowse our well spot that very afternoon. He said he'd only charge me ten dollars, seeing as how I was a friend of Doug and Wilma's, and he'd guarantee that if we didn't strike water right where he said, he'd return the ten dollars.

What was I to do? It seemed a fair bargain. Besides, despite my Illinois upbringing, I have always been a Missourian at heart. Until someone managed to "show me" that dowsing actually worked, I couldn't help but remain skeptical. *Here's my chance to do a little research,* I thought. *I'll just see where old Charlie says we should drop that well, then I'll get Frank over afterward and see how his prognosis checks out with Charlie's.*

So we piled into our vehicles and set out toward Summersville.

Sitting here now watching the play of afternoon sunlight on the rippling waters of the First Rocks pool, the skepticism I remember feeling as I drove home that day strikes me as a bit ironical. My life has been full of strange occurrences, and I take for granted much that many consider strictly supernatural. But to me faith is not a virtue. It divides people, neighborhoods, nations. I've often thought that if people were guided by their own experience, rather than by faith—in what others have told them—half the world's problems would likely disappear overnight. Even back then I made a point to distinguish between what I had learned through my own experience and various working hypotheses that I would test out from time to time. Until that day, I had no firsthand experience of water witching. I thought about it as I slowed the pickup and turned into our dirt road.

If Frank and Charlie both chose the same location for the well, it would provide some solid evidence that there was indeed validity to their art. Whereas if they witched totally different spots—as I half expected they would—and spoke of completely different underground streams, well then, it would prove once and for all that the whole thing was just hocus-pocus.

I had no foreboding of trouble as I accelerated up the final hill toward home, the others close behind. When we pulled into the yard, a dozen Greenwood School children had already assembled at the noise of our approaching vehicles. (Two at once was a rare occurrence.) Sherry soon joined us, and as we all gathered attentively around Charlie, it became evident that he would not only witch our well, but explain the process, step-by-step, as he proceeded.

Somewhere in his eighties, this renowned dowser seemed to live in a world where time flowed differently than in our own. I couldn't help but admire the way he lingered over his moments, taking time to experience them in depth. He moved slowly and deliberately, and spoke even slower still.

All eyes riveted on him as he led us to the edge of the forest and selected a wild cherry branch, explaining why it was the right shape and thickness. How it forked at just the right place. With his pocket knife he cut the branch from the tree and whittled its bark just so, pausing to test it from time to time until he was satisfied. He continued to whittle as he explained the importance of using green wood, ideally cut while its spring sap was still in flow.

When the cherry branch had assumed the classic Y shape prized by dowsers the world over, he handed it to me and told me to get the feel of it while he cut a counting stick. Still skeptical, I nevertheless felt as though I was in the presence of a master artisan.

"Countin' stick's a gotta be hickory," he drawled, getting the six words out in about the same time it'd take a New Yorker to rattle off directions to the Jersey Turnpike. "Just like y'r witcher's a gotta be cherry.

Oh, there's some that use other woods, but those
who know the business regard wild cherry as best for
y'r witcher, and hickory for y'r counter. Counter's
gotta be thicker'n y'r witcher in order to get the
count right. Don't need a Y for it—just a straight
branch'll do."

"What do you use it for?" I asked.

"Tell how deep your water lies, a course. When
you've found you a spot, you hold y'r counter over it
and she'll bob up and down, once for every foot you
got to dig. Forty bobs means y'r water's forty foot
down, eighty bobs, eighty foot, and so on."

Counting stick protruding from his back pocket,
wild cherry witching stick in hand, Charlie began to
walk solemnly across the parking area adjacent to the
house holding the Y-shaped branch before him.
Every now and then we'd see a significant twitch, accompanied by an audible gasp from those among his
audience who followed his movements with pure
hearts and guileless minds. In other words, everyone
but me . . . and possibly Doug.

"You got a small stream under here," Charlie said as
he inched his way toward the back of the house. "Can't
tell how deep it is yet. Runs over thisaway, cuttin' in
under the shed there, then headin' out into yonder
corn. There's probably another'n somewheres around.
If you're lucky, we'll find you a spot where two of 'em
cross. That'll be where you'll want to sink y'r well."

Watching Charlie move ever so slowly across the
lawn, I was beginning to wonder if he'd make it
around to the front of the house before dark when my
thoughts were interrupted by a familiar rattling.
Naw, it couldn't be, I thought. *Couldn't be . . .*

Seconds later my fears were confirmed.

Clanging up the hill, moving faster than I would
have thought possible, came Frank's truck. As he

pulled up in an ominous cloud of dust and Clyde reached out the window to work open her door from the outside, the door on Frank's side of the truck nearly exploded off. Before I had time to organize my thoughts into anything more coherent than a few silent expletives, Frank had leaped out and was walking toward us. Charlie's jaw dropped to the ground.

Frank faced me, witching stick in hand.

"Frank," I said in my most polite, matter-of-fact, nothing-out-of-the-ordinary's-going-on voice, "Frank, ah, this here is, uh, Charlie——"

"Aw, I know him!" Frank said, walking in front of his rival and waving a disgusted hand in his direction. "Knowed him a long time."

Without waiting for a reply, Frank walked assuredly across the yard, his witching stick in a business mode.

"You got you an underground stream runnin' right across here," he said, gesturing with his stick and walking so near to Charlie that I was afraid for a moment he might knock him over. Charlie still hadn't moved.

"Another'n runs along thisaway," Frank went on, walking rapidly across the yard, his witching stick twitching and nodding every which way—faster than any of us could possibly follow it.

"Runs up through where you got the grapes planted there 'n' drops down to run under this here tree 'longside the house. Then she takes off up through here——" he said, zipping diagonally behind Charlie, "'n' runs up thataway and on across over into y'r strawberry bed there."

Everyone except for Charlie walked briskly behind Frank as he swept around to the front of the house. "Here she takes off down along yonder fence for a spell and, let me see—yep, just what I thought. You got you another'n comin' up through here, then kinda anglin' off t' the northwest." Quickly he led us behind the house again where Charlie continued to stand motionless. "Let me see here, a couple a small'ns runnin' off under them little walnut trees back agin' the shed. They've a couple a minor trib-utrees, but this'n here's y'r strongest, that other'n runs a near second, they should cross somewheres around . . . yep," he concluded, using his boot heel to gouge out a bit of soil. "Here's the best spot to drill you a well."

After he had made the announcement, and taken a log from our nearby woodpile to mark the spot offi-cially, he turned to Charlie.

"No need *you* a-witchin' it! Best spot's right there. Besides, you can't witch no water with that cherry stick. Gotta be peach in this country."

Frank's assessment couldn't have taken more than two or three minutes. Of course, Clyde had once lived in this house and Frank was familiar with its grounds, so it was possible that he had witched it be-fore, whereas this was Charlie's first visit and—most probably, I thought while my mind raced for means of damage control—most probably his last.

Finally, after a silence so strained you could have cut it with a spatula, Charlie coughed a few times and began to show hints of returning life. Slowly the old man emerged from his trance, cleared his throat, pointed his witching stick to the ground, and said in his leisurely manner, "We-e-l-l, Fra-a-ank, you got that'n there right, and you got that yonder'n pretty close, a mite off, but near enough I s'pose—no more'n it matters—but you missed this'n altogether comin' up through here," gesturing as he said this and indi-cating the course with his stick.

"You gotta take this'n into account or you'll be steerin' the boy wrong. Lookee here," Charlie said, inching us slowly around to the front of the house where Frank had not spent as much time, and where Charlie soon indicated a stream Frank had failed to mention.

"I knowed about that," Frank snapped. "Too small to amount t' anything. Them other two streams that cross where I showed are both stronger'n this'n."

"This'n's stronger," Charlie countered, "near'n twice t'other."

"Wouldn't matter if it was," Frank shot back. "There's only a one a them. There's two a the others—and nearer the surface, too. Hand me that counter'n I'll show you."

Charlie yielded the counting stick, and we walked back to the spot Frank had selected. Everyone fell silent, watching as Frank held the stick in front of him. Soon it began to bob. As we watched and counted, the stick bobbed up and down eighty-eight times, then quit.

"You only got to go eighty-eight feet for this'n, Charlie. That other'n'll be much deeper. Go ahead, check it, you'll see."

And so they passed the next hour, critiquing one another's methods, concurring on some points, differing on others, arguing less vehemently as time went on, until at last, they both agreed on a spot for us to drill our well.

Charlie granted that Frank's choice had been a good one, but claimed this one was slightly better. Frank differed, politely, saying his first spot was better because it would give more water, but seeing as the water was a bit closer to the surface in this other one here, it'd do plenty good enough, and he reckoned

we'd be satisfied with it. In a touching display of una-
nimity, a somewhat reconciled Charlie picked up a
brick that was lying about and placed it on the
agreed-upon spot.

Frank fine-tuned it with a nudge of his boot. And
there it rested. On the dirt floor of our front porch. A
few inches from the wood stove where we did our can-
ning during July and August when it was too hot to
fire up the cook stove in the kitchen.

I was more relieved than I cared to admit at their
choice of location, for there was no way in hell anyone
in their right mind would ever—could ever—drill
there. The recommendation was one that I could, in
clear conscience, ignore. I knew (as I suspect Frank
and Charlie did as well) that operating a rotary drill
rig there would—well, to put it bluntly—reduce our
home to a pile of rubble.

Just to get the derrick in place I'd have to tear off
the porch, and by the time its two mammoth diesel
engines were cranked up and engaged in the business of driving a six-inch, carbide-steel bit through
four hundred feet of bedrock, the hundred-year-old
shanty we called home would quickly disintegrate
into a vibrating heap of kindling and twisted tin.

In the end neither Frank nor Charlie would accept
payment for their work, and Sherry's coffee and
homemade sassafras root beer took the edge off remaining tensions. That is, off *my* tensions. Everyone
else had had a grand old time. And the water witchers
themselves? The gleeful looks in each of the old boys'
eyes had explained it all as they had said their good-
byes. They had enjoyed every minute of it.

Since I planned to build an insulated enclosure
over the completed well, and intended to drill a hundred or more feet below the water table, I had in fact
already selected a convenient site behind the house.

To coincide with Frank's original recommendation, I had only to move my chosen site a few yards to the west. And there our well house sits today. Right where Frank witched it.

To the south of this pond where for some time now I have been sitting behind the arrowwood, a powerful grapevine stands out in a slant of afternoon sunlight. Although I often pass this way, I hadn't noticed it before. It twists from beneath the roots of a dogwood to encircle it in what at first appears a deadly embrace, its diameter larger than that of the tree upon which it grows.

Yet looking upward I see that the vine poses no threat. The dogwood, it turns out, is only its stair-step. When it reaches the tree's upper branches, it makes its way over into another, taller dogwood that it climbs until it can go no higher and then abandons it, too, for a taller oak. Brave choice, wise vine. It may kill the oak before my grandchildren are old enough to climb it, but this is an area where I allow nature to take her course.

Throughout this hollow that contains the First Rocks and spring, I limit my activities to jogging, observing, and occasionally cleaning up deadwood. I make no major alteration in nature's arrangements here. This—the heart of the forest—is her exclusive domain.

According to ancient Celtic folklore, every garden needs a "wild garden" in its midst "for the little people and nature spirits," a place undisturbed where herbs, weeds, and wildflowers can freely grow. Every farm, I feel, and every city, too, needs such a place at its heart—a wild area, kept free from development, a place left to fend for itself. But the ancient Celtic insight can be taken further.

To truly thrive, I believe, nations also require wild regions at their cores. Our state parks and national forests contribute to this, but I find it significant that the oldest mountains in our land (and among America's least developed forested areas) lie in the geographic center of our nation, and just a half hour's drive from the rapidly approaching U.S. population center.

Could these Ozark Mountains be America's wild garden? With their central Ozark National Scenic Riverways a sort of wild garden *within* a wild garden?

Even as the thought crosses my mind, I see it for the blatant regional chauvinism that it is, but all of us who love the land on which we live are guilty of it now and again. I will forgo describing how this farm lies in the geographic center of these ancient hills, how this creek bed centers the farm, and how the cliff from which gaze those stony countenances—well . . . a promise is a promise.

13

THIS IS NOT THE FIRST TIME I have seen the sunlight of late afternoon filter down through these trees to illuminate patches on the forest floor, some green, some brown, some wavering, some resting in silent stillness. Yet this is the first time the forest has ever looked like this.

The sun will not shine again at this angle until this precise minute of the hour one year from today. But conditions that day are not likely to duplicate this same amount of humidity, this same cloud pattern or air temperature. This is the first time I have walked *this* path, the first time I have seen *these* trees.

Oak, black walnut, sycamore, and hickory form a cathedral ceiling overhead; while nearer the ground, redbud, dogwood, cherry, and sassafras form a long corridorlike hall, adorning its walls with the stained glass and filigree of their new spring leaves. Maybe it's the time of day, or the season, but I sense something almost sacred beneath these trees. Perhaps it is always here, and my day in the forest has simply lifted the preoccupations that kept me from sensing it before.

It is hard to move with anything like speed along this path to the spring, for I know this daylight won't last. When I next pass this way, darkness will have wrapped its blanket round this part of the world. So I enjoy all I can, so long as the sunlight allows me to see.

Throughout the creek bed north of the path, witch hazel bushes thrive by the hundreds among rock and gravel in which few other plants seem able to grow. Witch hazel is the only plant in the forest to bloom in December and January. When all other foliage is bare, their yellow flowers unfold and release a glorious fragrance into the winter air, filling the hollow with a welcome reminder of spring.

When I first saw these bushes covered with yellow flowers one unusually warm January afternoon, I was concerned that the remaining frosts and snows of winter would discourage them. But witch hazel has a curious way of blossoming again and again throughout the winter, retreating on freezing nights, opening up again the moment the weather warms. Once I even saw them blossom with a foot of wet snow on the ground. Missouri has chosen the hawthorn as its flower, but for its resilient and indefatigable spirit, I've chosen the witch hazel as mine.

Jogging along this path can be tricky at times. Raking it regularly to keep it free of leaves has made it a haven for tiny wildflowers, and trying not to trample on them occasionally calls for some fancy footwork.

There are species of wildflowers here—and more than I have been able to identify—whose fully opened petals are no bigger around than the eye of a wood thrush. Some of them cluster along the edges of the path like miniature towns along a river's shore. If you do inadvertently step on them, they usually spring back readily enough, but at the moment it's no difficulty to step around this shamrock before me with its leaves of burgundy-streaked green and its tiny yellow flower. The step would have impressed it, I'm afraid—and a few others in its colony as well—

for the soil is still soft from the day's rain, and they cluster closely here. In fact the entire shamrock colony occupies an area small enough to be included in the umbrella shade of a single mayapple, which towers above them like a benevolent guardian tree.

Mayapples are not in the "tiny" category, growing to a foot or more in height. Like miniature palms, their leaves sprout upward from the top of each stem, and their fruit, when ripe, hangs coconut-style below. I have never known a mayapple to grow in solitude. The one growing here is part of a scattered and relatively small cluster of several dozen, but a bit further up the trail is a place where several hundred crowd together.

You have to be quick to sample the sweet, lemony fruit of these tropical-looking plants. The animals monitor their ripening with a jealous eye. As with so many other delectable fruits and berries of the wood, the forest creatures always seem to eat them the day before they are ripe.

Like stars interspersed in a sky of mayapple green, the blood-red flowers of a handful of fire pinks are scattered throughout. In the center of their little colony, a false Solomon seal reaches its starbursts of tiny white flowers so radiantly upward that a slight glow appears to hover about the entire plant—a plant that I feel should have a better name, for nothing about it strikes me as untrue.

West of the mayapples in a mini–river bottom of fertile, garden-quality soil, the earth expresses herself in the meaningful language of echinacea. Growing two to three feet in height, these are among Missouri's most beautiful and prolific wildflowers. Atop each stem a single daisylike flower points its purple petals downward from a central green disk bursting with orange stamens.

Common along roadsides throughout this area, *echinacea purpurea* has quite uncommon medicinal properties. A dose each morning and evening of a tincture made from steeping its root in a base of alcohol recently prevented my niece from contracting the measles despite unavoidable daily contact with a boy who had a severe case of them. And once, while I was on a speaking tour, the same tincture quickly rescued me from the potentially debilitating effects of a sore throat. Used by the Plains Indians more than any other medicinal herb, it is an excellent natural antibiotic and overall immune system enhancer.

A carpet of Houstonia bluets covers the last few feet of the path. Hundreds of these miniature blue flowers grow here, their stems no thicker than spider webs. Each of them has four tiny violet petals arranged around a white disk, centered with the merest speck of yellow. I step around them carefully to reach the open rock.

With the day's progression into early evening, the air has grown cooler. The sun's warmth feels welcome as I leave the shade of the forest and walk onto the open shelf of moss-covered limestone that forms the floor of this clearing above the spring. My body casts a long shadow across the area's geography as deliberately I inch forward, watching it glide across the curious features of the rock.

Looking down upon these formations in the evocative evening shadows, I find it easy to imagine that I am flying miles above a rugged landscape of wooded mountains and open arid plains. The clumps of moss look like forests of pine far below, and the gray stone resembles terrain I have looked down upon while flying over some of our western states. Here and there the gray is interspersed with circular patches of light-green lichen that bear an uncanny resemblance to the irrigated crop circles of this continent's fertile but moisture-hungry southwest.

Someday I'd like to photograph these rocks from this perspective, then give a slide show alternating their photos with aerial photos of the Sangre de Christos or Sierra foothills, challenging my viewers to tell the difference. During his slide presentation at one of IBM's annual meetings, a friend of mine once did something similar, following his slide of a magnified cancer cell with one of an aerial view of Los Angeles. He told me afterward that the IBM executives couldn't tell the difference.

What does Summersville look like from thirty thousand feet? Eminence? Mountain View? On the two occasions that I've flown over this area at that altitude, I could barely distinguish our local towns amid the rolling fields and forested hills that surround them.

To the north of these open rocks the hill is so steep that in places it qualifies as a small cliff. To speak of its "face" is especially appropriate, for like the cliffs in the wood between the worlds it is textured in a distinctly anthropomorphic manner, its little nooks and crevices forming a natural Abu Simbel of eyes, noses, lips, and furrowed brows.

The face of this cliff speaks of times quite different from our own. It has watched the sun from this location for more centuries, more millennia, than humans have existed on this earth. Erosion marks—where water seeping from the hillside trickles across it—must be four inches deep in places.

From tiny cracks and fissures such as these, wind, sun, frost, and rain create over the passage of ages crevices, gullies, streams, valleys, canyons—rivers and broad, fertile plains. It is beautiful to see the workings of these natural forces reflected in miniature all upon

the face of a single cliff—a monument to nature's pa-
tience as well as to her power.

Forty million years ago Mount Everest was low-
lying coastal shore; Kilimanjaro, not even a hairline
fissure in the plain of central Africa. Mount Fuji, even
now, has yet to complete its first *one* million years.
Yet this little cliff here is the exposed heart of a
mountain that has seen the suns, felt the winds, and
known the rains of 450 million years! Its history
stretches back into the almost-inconceivable depths
of a past when this planet's land masses huddled together in a single continent, and life on earth had not
yet left the oceans.

Nature has already moved the better part of this
mountain to the Gulf of Mexico, where its once snow-
covered summit now swirls as sand amid the coral,
plankton, and creatures of the warm saltwater sea.

The thought of moving an entire mountain fasci-
nates me now almost as much as it did when I was a
child—although then, of course, I thought of it in
very different terms. I was first presented with the
concept one Sunday when our pastor seemed determined to run the seventeenth chapter of Matthew not
just into the ground but right on through to the
earth's core.

Naturally my thoughts turned to the Himalayas.

I saw before me that glorious range, with all those
peaks to spare, and just as he was saying, *With faith
we can move them, any one of them* . . . I received what
seemed at the time a kind of revelation: It suddenly
became clear to me how much one of those peaks
would improve the quality of Cook County.

Religion took on sudden new meaning. There was
not a word I missed as the preacher concluded by em-
phasizing repeatedly while referring to some mountain or another that if we had sufficient faith, not

only *might* that mountain move, *it had* to move, by God. It had no choice in the matter, none at all but to trot on out of there when we gave the word.

I walked out of church determined to put the gospel into practice that very afternoon.

Considering my inexperience, I decided it best to start small and gradually work my way up. A seven-year-old, I thought, should at least be able to relocate a small hill. And I knew just the one. It stood in a vacant lot on the southwest corner of Mannheim and Forty-seventh Street, a twenty-foot-high mound of dirt where my friends and I would reenact historical battles—like Caesar's last stand against the Nazis and Custer's famous crushing of the Rubicon. After lunch I headed right over there and set about its removal.

When the mound failed to indicate the expected interest in travel, I lowered my sights to a nearby gravel pile. But although I applied myself to its relocation as assiduously as to any other task I tackled in those naive and energetic times, to my utter amazement—for I had plenty of faith—nothing happened. The Bible couldn't be in error. I must be doing something wrong.

When even the narrowing of my ambition to a slight lurch from a single piece of gravel failed to elicit so much as a quiver, I decided to attempt something easier. Nothing turned up for a week or so—and then one day at school I saw my chance.

A visiting parent had left a cigarette ash on one of the lunch tables. Exactly the sort of opportunity I had been hoping for. Surely a piece of fluff like that would respond to my thought. I focused my will upon it and commanded it to move. I *ordered* it to move. I ground my teeth, held my breath. I stared at the ash, I didn't stare. I completely relaxed and imagined it moving. I threatened, begged, reasoned, pleaded. Nothing. Nothing at all. As students congregated to watch this promising spectacle, under the mounting pressure I yielded to temptation. Quickly I snorted through my nose. A hot blast of air shot across the table; the ash moved—a full inch.

"You blew it!"

"No, I didn't either!"

"Yeah, you did too blow it. I saw you blow it."

One of the older students instantly became my heroine when she surprised everyone by saying, "He might not have blown it, you know; least I didn't *see* him blow it. It *could* have been his mind movin' it. I've heard of stuff like that."

Although I was later encouraged by some small achievements in this area, it was not until age fourteen that a high school science project brought me my first documented success.

Since it had proven so difficult to move inanimate objects solely through the power of thought, I decided to try my luck on something organic. Living things, I reasoned, can surely distinguish between love and hate, surely.

Spreading four inches of rich Wisconsin topsoil in an aquarium, I sowed it with grass seed, being careful to distribute the seed evenly throughout. Next I placed a glass divider down the aquarium's center, and painted a plus on the left side and a minus on the right. Setting the aquarium on a windowsill of the science room, I mounted behind it a poster outlining the goals of my project and asking everyone whose science class met there to send positive, loving thoughts toward the patch of dirt on the plus side, and ugly, hateful thoughts toward the patch on the minus side.

In addition to daily written records, I kept a bi-weekly photographic journal of the experiment's progress, beginning the first day with a photo of the two empty patches of dirt. Each day a classroom of witnesses watched as I watered the two sides equally. The sunlight streaming through the window showed no bias. Control factors in place, *thought* became the only variable . . . or so I reasoned, having not yet encountered the deep-seated prejudices of "objective" science.

As the weeks passed, the grass on the positive side of the aquarium came up thick and healthy, while only a few straggling shoots appeared on the negative side.

Participation in the project was infectious. Classmates would come in after school and work off steam by ranting and raving at the minus grass, while telling the plus grass how healthy and beautiful it looked. Every Monday and Thursday during the weeks preceding the science fair I would photograph the aquarium; and while first my science class then later the whole school watched in amazement, the grass on the plus side grew rich and luxuriant while the grass on the minus side remained thin and sparse.

Ignorant of the foregone conclusions that scientists must learn in order to become objective, I wrote up my hypothesis that mind affects matter and suggested that human thoughts and attitudes influence life-forms growing in their vicinity. I postulated the existence of an invisible mental and emotional climate and hinted that it might one day prove nearly as horticulturally significant as the physical climate.

When the day of the science fair arrived, I displayed the aquarium surrounded by posters outlining in neat block letters my hypothesis and methodology,

with references keyed to the text of my written report. The posters featured dozens of photographs
chronologically illustrating the progress and regress
of the respective patches of Kentucky blue.

The kids were impressed. Parents, too. My booth
drew large crowds and stimulated more discussion
than any other. The science teacher? As might be expected, he claimed it was all hocus-pocus. He even
went so far as to single out my project as "the least
scientific" of all the experiments that year.

My attempt to argue for a better grade soon made
it clear that I lacked the multiple-fact-firing verbal
skills needed to articulate a convincing pneumatic argument. Without one, chipping away at a mass of
petrified opinion was clearly impossible. With the
doors of the scientific community slammed in my
face, I exercised what seemed at the time my only
reasonable option. I bought a guitar, and reinvesting
my spirit of inquiry in a field that promised higher
dividends, joined a rock band.

My interest in the mental manipulation of physical
objects has long since given way to more relevant
themes. Yet looking at this little cliff today, and taking time to reflect upon my life, I realize that my
thoughts have in fact altered the physical world—and
far more than I would have once thought possible.
They have resulted in gardens, homes, barns, workshops, schools. Time and again I have seen them har-
ness tangible energies that went on to arrange real
events—some of lasting value, others just for enjoyment. I have imagined myself sailing a tall-masted
ship between tropical islands, tumbling with world-
class martial artists on the beaches of Japan, fishing
off the coast of Ireland, and sipping frothy stout in
sixteenth-century pubs. And I've lived to do all these

things and many others that seemed equally improbable when the thoughts first occurred. While my thoughts have not moved any outer mountains, they have helped this mountain I live upon to retain a thousand acres of its trees. And inspired me to spend this day among them.

While I have been standing here below the weathered cliff, the sun has slipped behind the first of the western trees that will soon extend their shadows across the whole of this rocky area above the spring. Unlike the First Rocks, this area has no lush island of greenery running through its midsection. Instead, between the Western Sea and the waterfall above the spring, a smaller pond has formed above a massive sheet of rock that slipped, probably centuries ago, into some underlying cave. The resulting basin catches both rainwater and water flowing into it from above. The water entering this central pool traces a slow circle around its banks before flowing outward toward the east, where it spills over the ledge in the waterfall, which still shows evidence of today's rain.

Warm steam rising from a sunny spot just above the waterfall issues a tempting invitation. Moments later I am comfortably stretched out on the warm limestone. Arms folded in front of me, chin resting on the back of my hands, my vantage point allows me to look down upon the water as it swirls briefly on a shelf of rock before tumbling into the spring basin.

After flowing rapidly down a terrace of glistening stones, the current pauses here in a whirling interplay of watery patterns, enjoying one last whirlpool before plunging into the Great Unknown.

This water enters a whole new world when it leaves the ledge, for the spring below marks the point where this creek ceases to be seasonal and becomes a bona fide year-round stream. Within hours this water will begin a series of rendezvous with other streams and rivulets, growing in breadth and depth, metamorphosing over coming weeks to become the Mississippi and, ultimately, the sea.

BEHIND ME, I HEAR the peepers along the banks of the Western Sea beginning to tune up for another of the jam sessions they schedule to concur with the twilight hours of these warm spring evenings. Their enthusiasm indicates that tonight's performance— titled, no doubt, "After the Rain"—will be something special.

Walking closer to better hear them, I inadvertently startle most of the soprano and all of the tenor sections. For a split second the pond resembles a pan of popping corn as the banks are vacated by dozens of airborne frogs leaping headlong into the water. While they dive for the substage anonymity of the pool's depths, I take a seat on the bank.

As time passes, one by one, they poke curious eyes above the water. I know that sooner or later one of them will tentatively "peep," to be followed in time by another, then another, until they are all peeping along again as lively as before. This may take some time, though, as it seems I've given them quite a fright.

Music buffs have not yet given frogs the credit they deserve for being among the most musically inclined of all the animals. No frog has yet been hatched from slimy gelatin mass who is not some sort of singer, croaker, crooner, or wart-wrapped rapper—

and the species known as "peepers" stands throat and gizzard above the rest.

Peepers live for music. Their entire lives are oriented around these evening concerts. They are so totally dedicated to music that they live where they do solely for the ambiance of the local sound—and for the company of others with similar audio preferences.

Human musicians, too, converge in places conducive to their type of music. Many live out their lives dedicated to a certain section of a particular city or even to some spot out in the middle of nowhere. I've known quite a number of musicians as rooted in their localities as indigenous flowers or trees. Like the sax player who lived down the hall from us on Chicago's south side. It was hardly what you'd call luxury accommodations, but the rent was cheap. Thirty-three dollars per month secured us a fourth-floor room with access to a shared kitchen and bath; and despite racial tensions elsewhere, not once did any of our neighbors make us feel uncomfortable for being the only white family in the building. Several even went out of their way to make us feel at home. Our two preschoolers had no shortage of playmates, and in the musically rich atmosphere—somebody was always blasting something—we enjoyed the comfort of a happily extended family.

While for most, residency at 6106 South Ellis was a way of life, for Sherry and me it was just a stepping stone, a place to earn some money convenient to the University of Chicago bookstore where I worked and the nearby hospital where Sherry was employed as a nurse's aide.

Yet there were several musicians living in that building who could have probably afforded elegant homes on the north side had their dedication to sound been less complete. They lived in our building because they wanted to, because it kept them close to the Chicago blues scene. To them, St. Louis and New Orleans were but pale imitations. Chicago was where it was at—and God help anyone who tried to tell them otherwise.

Each month Sherry and I would salt away a few more pieces of camping equipment and a little gas money. When we had saved enough to make it cross country, we headed west for the hills above Big Sur, where a different sort of music pervaded the air.

There, in a certain campground in Los Padres National Forest, I hoped to meet up with another musician, a friend named Salty, who used the campground as his primary interface with civilization, camping there long enough to barter for his needs, then disappearing again into the hills, where madrone, manzanita, California bay laurel, and pin oak formed his preferred acoustic ambiance. I had left him in the middle of a bizarre adventure and was naturally curious as to how it had turned out.

Salty earned his strings and bread digging for gold.

Somewhere far back in the national forest's maze of uninhabited hills, far from any roads, he had staked and legally registered a claim for a gold mine. He and a few others had discovered a strange quirk in a federal mining law that dated back to the nineteenth century and had never been officially taken off the books. Under this law, prospectors would be granted legal title to twenty acres of land if they registered their claim, lived on it for five years, and brought a certain minimum amount of gold into the county assay office each month to prove that it was indeed active.

Although Salty's claim was on national forest property, and park service regulations prohibited "camping" in the same spot for more than two weeks, if he could somehow get away with living on his mining claim for five years (while proving that he was extracting that monthly minimum of gold) the older nineteenth-century law would take precedence and award him full legal title to the land—and there wouldn't be a thing the park service could do about it.

Meanwhile, however, the park rangers had legal authority to order Salty off his claim anytime they caught him there. They knew exactly *what* he was up to, but they were not sure *where*.

Periodically they would hunt for him using jeeps and sometimes even helicopters. But in those days before government records were so thoroughly computerized—and with rivalry between different branches of government being what it is—the rangers had no way to get their hands on Salty's official claim papers to find out exactly what acreage he was claiming. It was classic cat and mouse, better than anything I have encountered in fiction, and my wily, gray-bearded friend thrived on it.

I was one of a handful of people whom he trusted enough to bring to his claim site. Far back in the hills, his mining shack was camouflaged beneath the branches of living trees and so cleverly concealed in the tuck of a hollow that it was impossible to spot from the air. He built fires of only the driest wood and took other precautions that had so far succeeded in helping him escape detection.

When I had last seen him just over a year earlier, Salty had been working his claim for three and a half of the requisite five years. If he was still at it, he would need to escape detection only a few more months to be awarded his land. But I had another reason for wanting to see him again: his music.

In the quiet of the evenings and late into the nights, Salty played the sitar. He was as dedicated to that spot there in the California hills as the blues musicians were to Chicago, as dedicated as these frogs are to this pond.

Like these peepers—who are now beginning to warm up again—Salty's life revolved around his music. He was living his furtive, outlaw existence not because he cared about gold or lusted after land but because he had found a certain spot in the high dry hills where the naturally occurring acoustics were ideally suited to his unique and haunting style of music. It was a place where by day the bees spoke to him through the droning sounds they made in the hollow log instruments that were their homes—logs, he claimed, they had chosen for their acoustics.

When he and I would get to talking music, as we often did around his campfire, he would explain to me how by day he was learning the language of the bees, and by night, the language of the stars. He had mastered, he said, the basics of both languages but would require many more years, perhaps even the rest of his life, to acquire the ability to converse with the fluency he desired. I did not understand everything he explained—and admittedly some of it was a bit difficult to take merely on faith—but it was clear that his only reason for wishing to own the land, which did indeed yield a small amount of gold, was so he could settle down and pursue his musical vision undistracted.

Often after playing a long and haunting melody on his sitar, Salty would pause in the late-night stillness and listen. Several times during such pauses he claimed to be hearing the music of the stars.

I heard it only once myself, but that was enough to make me a believer. I had been looking off into the Milky Way, the music of Salty's sitar drifting in and out of my thoughts, when suddenly I heard a different sound. It was a kind of loud drumming hoofbeat that began in one part of the sky, slowly moved across to the other, and then oscillated back and forth, echoing, as if the whole sky had become a pair of headphones and someone were playing with the balance.

Salty was used to it, but it terrified me. Perhaps now if I was to hear it again I might react differently, but I was deeply shaken at the time. It was an impossible sound, a sound that logic knew could not exist unless made by something so large and vast that my friend and I were but motes of dust in comparison. I can think of no recorded music with which to compare this uncanny hoofbeat drumming, except maybe some Kalahari drum chants a friend once played for me.

Yet oddly enough, although the sounds these peepers make are poles apart from what Salty claimed were the sounds of stars, their music is structurally quite similar, almost as if these little water creatures here are playing the same song on very different instruments. Since they seem to have recovered now, with one last thought of Salty—whom I never did meet up with again—I turn my attention to their fevered and more familiar music. Gently I join the chorus of happy chirping, whistling a few carefully timed peeps of my own.

Most people assume that frogs are primarily oriented toward water. They are not. Frogs are primarily oriented toward sound. What really prompts an Ozark frog, what makes him get up in the morning and keeps him awake far later into the night than is good for him, is music. To a frog these evening jam sessions are rock concert, world series, and revival meeting all rolled into one.

I made the discovery by accident one night when our cow failed to show up for milking and I was out under the stars leading her in toward the barn. We were passing near a little dugout where some long-ago farmer with a horse and plow had made one of those quick, make-do-for-now ponds that you form by running your plow in the same direction to build up one bank, then turning around and building up the other in the same way until you have scooped out a shallow basin that will fill up when it rains.

This particular little dugout is dry most of the year. But there are a few weeks here and there—usually in spring when rains are plentiful—when water covers an oblong area about twenty feet across, not even as wide, and hardly more than ankle deep. So I was surprised, bringing in Bossie that night, to hear coming from this little mud hole the sounds of a major frog fest.

Walking over to investigate, I discovered what must have been, or at least what sounded like, a hundred or more frogs, toads, and whatnot, all carrying on at once. That little glorified mud puddle was crowded with every kind of peeper and croaker you can imagine, and it just didn't make sense. A much larger pond lay only a few hundred feet away—no more than a hop, skip, and a jump to a frog. Why weren't they down there?

Even at its liveliest I had never heard the larger pond host a gathering of this magnitude. I walked down there to verify, and sure enough, despite a volume of water hundreds of times greater, I heard only a handful of dull and unambitious frogs. Apparently all but the sick and elderly had moved up to this little puddle near the barn. For months afterward I noticed that whenever that mud hole had even so much as an inch of water in it, frogs congregated there by the score.

When you don't have television or radio, you've got a lot more time on your hands in the evenings, so one night when my curiosity was at a peak and so were the frogs, I decided to go out there and sit by the edge of the water until I got to the bottom of it. And I soon did.

That puddle had an echo—and a surprisingly powerful one at that.

Somehow the way it is banked up to face the flat wall of the farmhouse—two hundred feet to its west— causes an audio ricochet. Every single note those frogs let loose bounced back at them two, three, sometimes even four or five times. By the time you had a whole chorus of frogs and peepers all carrying on at once, those echoes made it sound like every frog in six counties had come—and brought his family, too.

Listening from the edge of that little pond, I realized that the sounds were not random. They had a distinct pattern and cadence. Even their offbeats were regular and consistent. Many nights after that I sat by the edge of the water listening to their music. When I finally joined in with my own whistling, I imitated the peepers' calls so closely they failed to notice its non-frog origin.

Temptation being what it is, and I no less mortally curious than the next, I was soon wondering if I could teach them a few variations. Their considerable talents had all been channeled into the overperfection of a single song. I naturally applauded the piece, for I recognized in it the fundamental rhythmic patterns that have given birth to virtually all of America's indigenous music. The problem was, the frogs hadn't changed this song since they crawled from the Devonian swamps. And, by God, there is such a thing as evolution.

After dozens of hours of whistling in their repetitious choruses, I wanted to both show off a bit and, if possible, thrust the local frog sound to new heights, doing all I could to help it bust on through the peduncle of that single tune into the more innovative sphere of the next musical phylum. What that new sound would be for a frog, only nature knew, but I was sure it would be an improvement.

After 350 million years topping the amphibious music charts it seemed possible that the song's initial appeal might be wearing thin—at least among certain of the younger and more progressive frogs, of which the peepers were clearly the vanguard. Maybe even this very night they were poised upon the threshold of some major musical mutation—and I could be its catalyst. The idea held a certain appeal.

Carefully I began to introduce slight variations into their relentless ancestral theme. I did it so subtly at first that they never once suspected it was not coming from just another, well—I'll be candid—I hoped they would think of me as a sort of superfrog, but a frog nonetheless. My goal was to draw them into newer and deeper levels of vocal development, to stretch them to the very limits of their capabilities, inspiring and encouraging them as would any effective coach. Yet in no way did I seek to humble them or tempt them with a song (or songs) hopelessly beyond their ability.

Within that self-imposed moral framework, whistling that fine line, I have jammed with frogs lo these many years now, and I think it fair to say that I approach tonight's festivities with some degree of skill. For example, I've learned that on any given night each peeper can peep only one note. To peep a different note requires either the growth of their bodies, which does occur as the weeks pass, or, oddly enough, a change in water or air temperature.

Yet while each peeper here tonight is able to peep only its one given note, taken all together, they cover a considerable range. Half-note, whole-note, sometimes even a dozen or more half-note differences exist between the pitch of one peeper and the next, which is to say, on a good night a chorus of peepers might achieve through collective effort what any human being could accomplish by just casually whistling a tune.

My years of jamming with frogs have taught me that there is an optimal pattern they try to achieve, a goal, you might say. Whenever they achieve this pattern, which goes something like this—

peeeeep peeeeep peep peep peep peeeeep peeeeep

—they begin singing for all they are worth, and are sometimes able to maintain it for a relatively long while (three minutes, forty-five seconds seems to be average).

Not until this optimal pattern has been established and running smoothly for a minute or more do the bullfrogs join in with their deep-throated brrruuubit-brrruuubit, brrruuubit-brrruuubits. And should it progress to that grand and glorious point where eight or ten bullfrogs are barking alongside chorus frogs, cricket frogs, scores of peepers, miscellaneous toads and others, what usually happens is that everyone gets so excited by the wild, raucous, foot-stomping sound that somebody—and it is usually a young tree frog—misses a beat.

Then everyone loses it, and they have to start all over because the bullfrogs won't join back in until the rest of them have the tune humming along fairly well again. (Being both the most dignified and the most conceited of the singers, bullfrogs are not only last to join in but also first to quit when mistakes are made.)

Since I know in advance precisely to what musical heights these creatures aspire, and since my advanced human biocircuitry enables me to simulate the essence of their hoped-for collective results, I am in a unique position to accelerate the process by which they achieve it. And once they do, I am able to help them stabilize that optimal pattern and continue it longer than usual. It is then that my real work begins: the introduction of the subtle variations that form the core of my curriculum.

Whoever said "You can't learn a frog" was but an amateur in this field. You most certainly can. The secret, of course, is to think like a frog. To do this, one must enter wholly into their frivolous spirit. Many novices become alarmed at this point and cling to their inhibitions, but wise in the ways of frogs, I relax into the spirit of the evening, having learned long ago that frog fests are no place for serious thought.

I begin by peeping the same note over and over again, establishing myself as a certain frog, sitting in the vicinity of a certain presumed bush in the dark— a frog, just like all the other frogs.

Only after they have fully accepted me as one of their own do I accelerate things by getting right to the

peeeeep peeeeep peep peep peep peeeeep peeeeep

point that represents for them the summit of collective achievement. When the desired rhythmic pattern appears so early in the proceedings, a congratulatory buzz circulates among the assembly, carrying with it a sense of heightened certainty that it will indeed be a good night. The bullfrogs bark in, enthusiasm gushes forth, and everyone contributes something. The more daring of the crowd even flirt on the edges of improvisation.

However, this is where I have to be extremely careful. Prior experience has shown me that if the level of enthusiasm becomes excessive, the frogs will mess it up—every time. So I carefully back off for a while, returning to repetitive peeps of the same note, planning

to continue them for as long as it takes to establish
the slow and steady building that insures against pre-
mature crescendo and subsequent crash.

Several minutes pass. I struggle to be patient.

Finally, sensing the arrival of the right moment, I
venture further, continuing my repetitions of the
same—

peeeeep peeeeep ₚₑₑₚ peep peep peeeeep peeeeep

—pattern, but quietly, subtly, transforming them
into a progression, sliding the third repetition up five
half-steps, slipping back down with the fourth. When
that fifth repetition rolls around, I go for it, shooting
on up seven half-steps, whistling two long peeps, then
dropping down two half-steps for a couple more before resuming my whistling of the basic pattern just
as it began. The whole thing goes something like this:

If you ever want to really blow a frog's mind, try
whistling this sometime. Pull over one dark night
when you are driving past a good-sized pond, slide on
up there to the water's edge, and give it your best
shot. Even though the frogs can't see you as you are
whistling this, you can feel them out there in the dark
practically worshiping you. It's cheap therapy. Quickest way I know to pump up a flagging self-esteem.

My whistling of this progression has continued for
several minutes now. The frogs are really getting

down; the pond is buzzing; there's electricity in the air. It feels like something is about to gel. I know it's wrong, but temptation overpowers me and I shift it into a rock mode, dropping in a little Led Zeppelin and a couple of Grateful Dead riffs. It works! The frogs just eat it up. In fact things are going so well, I ease back into the basic progression and—while continuing to whistle—ponder the pros and cons of attempting something I have only pulled off once before without causing them all to fall silent. But what a feeling that one time it worked! I felt like I had done to those frogs what that monolith in Clark's *2001* did to those apes: I whistled George Frideric Handel's Courante in G (from Suite no. 14).

During the decade we lived without electricity and electronically reproduced sounds, our evenings were often filled with Sherry's playing of Handel's music on the piano. During that time I perfected the whistling of this excellent baroque ditty, which to this day remains my favorite piece of keyboard music.

As in so many of his compositions, in this courante Handel captured something unspeakably joyful and optimistic, something Bach, Scarlatti, and others of the period also touched upon, but that no one captured so consistently as or expressed more powerfully than Handel. And not just in his *Messiah*, which personally I do not consider his best work, but in dozens of lesser known compositions like Passacaglia, Larghetto, Allemande, the Air and Hornpipe from the *Water Music*, and others too numerous to mention.

Handel's music acted upon the thought of his age like sunlight upon a flower, drawing out the budding idealism, the dormant hope and vision of those who were troubled by the political excesses of their monarchs, and by colonial policies that in their times had become more brutal than any the world had ever known.

As it was played throughout the capitals of Europe, his music and the music of the many composers it inspired became rallying points for a growing body of open-minded thinkers whose writings began to explore the ideals of freedom, liberty, and for the first time in Western history, basic human rights. Coupled with the printing press, this set in motion the tide of populist thinking that later in that pivotal eighteenth century would produce the American and French revolutions.

In the end, Handel's music became a principal catalyst in the birth of the democratic movement. The same movement that even now continues to shape our world. And of all his music, nowhere did this man whom Bach considered "the greatest composer of the age" convey that sense of hope and possibility, that impetus to shake off the shackles of the past and forge ahead into a new and higher order, nowhere did he convey the raw power of that irrepressible democratic spirit more compellingly than in this courante.

This is why it was so unfair to whistle it to the frogs.

Introducing something within the range of their comprehension but so infinitely beyond their capacity to reproduce was, I'll admit, a little hard to justify. But after hundreds of millions of years cheeping the same old tune, surely, I thought, they must be poised at the edge of a breakthrough. Handel's courante could be just what was needed to push them over the edge. Besides, I was curious whether or not they'd appreciate it.

Sitting there under the influence of the frogs' devil-may-care frivolity, it had even occurred to me that their emotional response to eighteenth-century chamber music might shed some light on our own human situation. After all, what *was* the reality that Handel translated into music? If people were too cerebral, too oriented in the deeply rutted pathways of left-brain logic to see it, well, damn it, maybe the frogs wouldn't be. Maybe they would see something, feel something, grasp something that we had missed. I concluded that Handel was worth whistling that long-ago night, and I decide to risk it again now, with this year's frogs.

Their singing has been strong and steady for some time. The courante's initial notes flow easily into the stream of their well-established rhythm. Their steady, earthy croaks underline the cascading waterfalls of the ingenious melody of Handel's courante as it dances a staccato staircase through the scales, tumbling through one happy possibility, exploding into another, and yet another again.

Blending this musical pattern of the long-ago 1720s with tonight's peeper pattern, older still, I plunge wholeheartedly now into my whistling recitation of Handel's finest.

The frogs sing in new and unprecedented patterns. For a few perfect moments, it is as if some enlightened forest muse embraces us in an audible glory. The enthusiasm rises. Long-standing Devonian beliefs are called into question as certain of the younger frogs begin to suspect that the term *song* may have a plural form. The pool and all its little singers are lifted as every peeper and hoary frog tries to exceed its best, singing better, then better still. Unfortunately, so do I.

Carried away, I overplay my part.

First one, then another peeper drops out until a reverent hush falls over the assembly, and I am left whistling in the dark, alone. There is but one thing to

do when this happens: Return to square one and resume the time-honored pattern

peeeeep peeeeep peep peep peep peeeeep peeeeep

But since I'm only human . . .

I first treat the frogs to a complete and uninter-
rupted rendition of the song that brought such glory—
and such defeat. Then, since they seem so appreciative,
I continue, whistling Allemande, Passacaglia, and Air
from the *Water Music.* In the stunned silence that follows, compassion compels me to take a few minutes to
reassure the dazed amphibians with a string of simple
peeps, followed by a few minutes of:

peeeeep peeeeep peep peep peep peeeeep peeeeep

peeeeep peeeeep peep peep peep peeeeep peeeeep

peeeeep peeeeep peep peep peep peeeeep peeeeep

Not until my little friends are again joined in enthusiastic chorus do I steal quietly across the rocks
for a final drink at the spring and a few silent moments beneath its restful roof of stone.

I ENJOY THE QUIET LUXURY of sitting beneath the massive rock ledge that overhangs the spring. The air is always cool here in the perpetual cavelike shade, and the surrounding stone creates a calm, reflective atmosphere that I find a refreshing contrast to the festive excitement of the peepers and their merry singing.

Beside my stone seat, the water (barely visible in this twilight hour) flows from three distinct crevices in the rock, each of which seems to be the favorite for a time as the tides of seasons ebb and flow. I make it my work, especially when drought is upon us and water scarce, to nurture carefully these three sources of the spring, cleaning out debris with my hands and deepening the channels down which the water flows to pool just above a little stone-and-gravel dam. It is not a large dam that I have built here—it rises only about six inches—but it is enough to trap a basin of water at whose deepest point I have buried one end of a three-quarter-inch galvanized pipe.

The pipe runs horizontally beneath the dam, ending twelve feet away in a graceful curve that delivers a consistent stream of water, easy to situate a jug beneath or steady a hand upon when kneeling for a drink.

Seven feet of solid rock separate the heat of the daytime sun from the stream that emerges here. But

the water itself originates deep within the surrounding hills in countless subterranean tricklings that
keep it at a cool, fifty-eight-degree temperature year-
round.

I have never seen this spring run dry, although
during the drought of 1977 it slowed to such a trickle
that in order to fill our five-gallon jug we had to leave
it overnight and come back for it in the morning.
Some claim that water from a spring such as this is
unfit for drinking because it may have passed
through underground caverns, where it could have
picked up bat guano, thereby becoming a source of
disease. Yet I know for a fact that generations of settlers have thrived on this water, as did countless native generations before. And for nearly a decade the
entire moisture content of my body came from it, too.
I'll consider it no great risk to drink my fill before I
set out for home.

From the cave beneath this ledge I look out upon a
twilight world framed by living stone. With my eyes
now adjusted to peering from darkness into twilight,
it feels as though I am within some geologic camera,
looking through an aperture of stone upon a world all
the more beautiful for its rugged frame.

Maybe because my day has been spent outdoors, in
a forest without artifacts to anchor my perception—
and since dawn my thoughts have been free to roam
without reference to others—I am more able now to
see into the essence of things.

Increasingly I find myself catching glimpses of luminous patterns in the air, shimmering hints of the
invisible currents of cause within and behind the visible world. Over the years I have watched these aerial
patterns late into many a night. While all of them do

not fall into this category, I have come to recognize most of them, and certainly the ones I see before me now, as the objectified thoughts of nature.

When we think of intelligence, we naturally think in terms of human intelligence, but intelligence takes many forms. Science describes the sun's interaction with the earth—and the mechanisms through which it produces life—in terms of countless separate processes, systems, laws, properties, tendencies, all of which are valid. But in the course of analyzing the components, we often lose sight of the whole. Earth and sun are not without intelligence.

The native American who speaks of mother earth and father sun is aware of this simple yet profound truth. And with that truth as premise, logic is able to proceed along pathways closed to those who see only the material or technical side of life. Often these pathways offer the most direct routes to insights that are vital to our understanding of this earth and its ecology—and essential if we are to offer it proper care.

To me it makes sense to regard the earth and the sun as sources of two very different forms of intelligence. In the earth's biosphere they weave together to form the mind of nature. Those who are open to looking at things this way find that a sort of window opens before them. Through this window I've seen some interesting things. While I do not claim to un-derstand all of them, there are fundamentals of which I am certain. Nature, for example, thinks in a lan-guage of geometry, and creates through geometric form.

Just as in my mind I envision a building before I build it, this earth, this creek bed, this forest around me were also envisioned before they took form.

Everything I see, everything I perceive, everything that my senses interpret—every sound, every nuance of light, all that I feel, smell, taste, the air I breathe—first existed as a mathematical possibility. As nature turned her attention to certain of these possibilities, they slowly began to take form, and from the same invisible realm that long before had given birth to matter, organic life was born.

This invisible realm is the organizing substructure of the visible. It is the same dimension of "thought frequencies" that native Americans call the spirit world, from which country people derive their second sight, and from which all of us get our occasional flashes of intuition.

While twilight holds motionless my cave-framed view of the forest, I see many of these visions that nature is holding. Some have existed in this basin for such lengths of time that trees, shrubs, moss, and other life-forms have conformed to their contours and taken on their shapes. Some have left as deep an impression in the limestone that forms this cave as the Ordovician ocean waves whose ripples on the sand of some long-forgotten shore still show petrified on the underside of the ledge above me. When I am still, they brush the periphery of my awareness, and as my wordless attention focuses upon them, their geometric essences emerge clearly defined, suspended before me in the air.

As a child I saw this geometric content of the air regularly, not just under circumstances as ideal as today's, but most of the time. Whenever I cared to pay attention to it, it was there. Like many children, I took the existence of an invisible world for granted, assuming it just as real as the world of sight and sound. I lived in both worlds, thinking they were one and seeing no conflict. It never occurred to me to talk much about it. I assumed that everyone was aware of it much as I was.

One night at the age of four I learned otherwise. Whoever had done the mudding and taping of the sheet rock walls of my bedroom had lacked Sherry's skill. In an upper corner where the sheet rock met the planks of the exposed wood ceiling, they had left a tiny hole through which light from the kitchen entered my room. Each night as I lay in bed I would enjoy watching a procession of geometric patterns tunnel into and out of that pinpoint of light.

I remember the squares the best—the four directions, the four elements of the ancient alchemists, the four forces of the physicists—but there were also circles, triangles, and sometimes complex structures that I couldn't name. I saw these patterns during the day as well, but it was usually at night, when the day's brightly colored distractions were behind me, that I entered most fully into their world.

My door was shut that night; the room was dark. I had been in bed for some time, watching slowly rotating concentric squares tumble into tunnels that disappeared off into the infinite distance of that single point of light, revolving all the while like images on some yet-to-be-invented computer screen. Hearing my father walking past my door, on impulse I called to him. He came into the room and sat down on the side of my bed.

"What is it, Kenny?"

"What are those squares you see all the time?"

"Those what?"

"You know, those little squares you see all the time that are always going in and out of each other."

It wasn't anything my father said that alerted me to the fact that something was wrong. It was my sense that he had become afraid.

"I don't know what you're talking about," he said, a little too hastily. "I don't see any squares. Go to sleep. You're imagining things."

That was the last inquiry I made of adults. I did put out a few tentative feelers to my sister, Marianne, and to my playmates. Unlike my father, my peers did not seem to find the subject troubling—and they seemed to know what I was talking about—but their attention spans, like mine in those early years, were on the lean side of brief. With no language to describe my impressions and no one with whom to discuss them, my awareness of the invisible geometry of the world slowly receded behind a world increasingly defined by report cards, homework, and growing responsibilities. But this awareness did eventually return, and in some dramatic ways.

Not long after I had launched into my adult life, incidents began to occur that convinced me that my childhood sensings had been correct, that an invisible world did indeed interpenetrate the world of sight and sound. As evidence of its existence began cropping up in my life, I was quick to see that familiarizing myself with it might very well lead to certain practical advantages. With a family to support, this possibility so piqued my interest that it began for me a study of the subject that continues to this day.

Of the many remarkable incidents that demonstrated to my young adult self both the existence and the influence of an invisible realm, two stand out above all others. Had they not occurred I would have spent these past decades elsewhere.

Listening to the sounds of today's rainwater splashing on the spring basin's rocky floor, my thoughts drift back to the first of these incidents. I was listening to the sounds of another rain splashing on the cab of the truck I was driving. Beside me in the front seat were Billy, age five, Valarie, age three, and Sherry, then pregnant with Becky.

We had been living for some months in a cabin on an old turn-of-the-century homestead, twelve miles outside Camptonville, California. We had rented the place for its beauty and quiet seclusion, not suspecting how difficult it would be to find work in so sparsely populated an area. When money ran out, we sold our only possession of any value—an old but dependable vehicle. Half the money went for a sixteen-year-old pickup truck. With the other half we bought groceries, gardening tools, and three more months in what we considered a virtual paradise. But when summer's end found us down to our last fifty dollars, Sherry and I had to accept the inevitable: We could not stay.

Our dream was to establish a meaningful, long-term relationship with the earth. For that, a piece of land that we could call our own was essential. To earn the money to purchase that land, I needed to find a job at which I could work steadily for the next few years.

Since Chicago, where I had my best employment connections, was half a continent away, we thought next of Berkeley. During the few months we had lived in this bustling Bay Area college town, I'd had no problem finding work. It was the logical place to start my job search. But while considerably nearer than Chicago, it was still a hilly two hundred miles to the southwest, and soon after purchasing my sixteen-year-old truck I discovered that it burned two quarts of oil for every tank of gas—and had a rod knocking that could cripple the engine at any time. Our decision to bolt on its homemade wooden camper shell and set out with all our possessions was irrevocable.

For better or for worse, that truck would be our home until I found work.

North of Point Reyes Station, Highway 1 runs along the rim of a cliff several hundred feet above the Pacific coast. Even long after sunset, the dramatic contrast of great heights and plummeting depths could still be felt in the cab of the truck as we followed the winding road southward.

Noticing that we had used half a tank of gas, I pulled over to put in another quart of oil and stepped out into the blowing rain of a night as black as this forest will be in an hour or so. Opening the hood, I set the flashlight on the fender and repeated the familiar ritual. Far below me, I could hear the rumbling pulse of breakers crashing on the shore.

It swept over me so quickly I had no time to identify it—a surge of emotion so powerful, in a moment it had me feeling as though I were tottering at the edge of an inner precipice that bore an uncanny resemblance to the outer one. Somewhere down there, below the surface of my conscious thought, I felt a turbulent sea of emotion pounding relentlessly upon the basis of my self-worth. Troubled waves—of what emotion I could not be sure—seemed intent on breaking through to engulf my awareness.

Something within me was about to explode. It was too much pressure, responsibility, uncertainty. Living out of a truck had made it clear to me just how much two trusting children and a pregnant wife looked to me for food, clothing, and shelter. Down to our last twenty dollars, our only possession of any value exchanged for a near-worthless truck that was now our home, I felt that I had failed Sherry, the children. They deserved better.

It was past midnight, and we still had several hours of driving ahead. When the last of the oil had drained from the can, I slammed down the hood and began to climb back into the truck, but I was finding it nearly impossible to hold back whatever it was within me that seemed to be demanding expression. While I knew Sherry would understand—she always did—I did not want to frighten the children. Telling her not to worry, I explained my need for a few minutes alone.

"I'm going to pray along the cliffs," I said. "I'll be back soon."

I had barely left the cab when the floodgate opened in earnest. Sobbing without restraint—as if some primitive animal mechanism had taken over—I walked toward the breakers, instinct guiding me through darkness toward the sea. Partway down the cliffs, I stood on a protruding rock, lifted my arms to the stormy sky, and prayed in a voice loud enough to drown out all other sound.

With a passion that felt strangely warm and healing I shouted my words into the sky above the pounding surf, asking the Creator to help me provide a better life for the people I loved, to help Sherry and me secure the stewardship of some land where we could raise our children, plant trees, and live to see both children and trees mature, a place where we could grow our own food and do our best to live out the remainder of our lives in harmony with God and nature.

My outpouring had ended and I was near exhaustion when I felt a shift in air pressure as though something had moved across the sky. The weight that had been with me for days suddenly lifted from my heart. In its place came a passionate resolve. I *would* get that job. I had to. In darkness I made my way back to the truck, determined to find work. First thing in the morning.

Hours later I pulled into a quiet residential street in the Berkeley Hills, being certain—since the truck had no emergency brake—to park on a level spot. After blocking the tires, I crawled in back with the others, hoping to get some sleep. The rain was falling harder now, blowing the canvas we had tacked across the open back of the camper shell.

Sherry and I both knew that we were at a cross-roads that night. Experiences like this either strengthen or destroy; there is no middle ground. The canvas was no match for the unusually heavy September downpour, but our relationship was. We awoke the next morning cold and damp, but closer than ever.

Groggily I opened the tailgate and set up the Coleman stove. Sherry began preparing coffee and oatmeal, trying not to draw attention from the well-dressed commuters who glanced at us curiously as they walked past on their way to work. After breakfast we drove down into one of Berkeley's business districts, where I stopped at a gas station. In its restroom I washed, shaved, brushed my teeth, and put on my only clean shirt. I was as ready as I would ever be. To Sherry I said what she already knew, "No point looking for a place to live until I have a job, or at least the promise of one. I don't want to live anywhere I can't find work. If I can't find a job here . . . " I hesitated, reluctant to go on. But the reassuring hand she placed on my arm made it clear I needn't continue.

"Don't worry," she said. "You'll find one. Just take it a step at a time." I could see that she believed what she said.

Since some years earlier I had worked as a mail carrier in Hinsdale, Illinois, the post office was the logical place to start my job search. I parked in front of the YMCA across from the main Berkeley office. While Sherry and the children waited in the truck, I

entered the building and climbed the stairs to the
second-floor personnel office. A friendly, round-faced
man greeted me from behind a cluttered desk. I told
him that I was looking for work.

"Name?" he inquired abruptly. I made my reply.

"Spelling, last name?"

"Uh, Carey, C-A-R-E-Y."

"Carey . . . Carey . . . " he mumbled, flipping pages
and running a finger down columns of computer
print. Suddenly he looked up, a puzzled expression
on his face, "Carey?" he asked, "Kenneth Xavier
Carey?"

Surprised that he knew my full name, I nodded a
brief affirmative.

"What are you doing here now? It's only half past
ten. Your appointment isn't until eleven-thirty."

"My appointment?" I stammered, incredulous. "I
have an appointment? An hour from now?"

"Yes, yes, after evaluating your score on the Civil
Service Test you took last year in Oakland, we sent
you a letter. You should have received it months ago.
It told you to be here today at eleven-thirty for your
interview. We have other applicants scheduled now.
You'll have to come back in an hour."

"No problem," I said, explaining that I had moved
and not received the letter. "I'll be back. You can
count on it."

Euphoric falls short of describing how I felt as I
walked out of that building. I knew I had the job. A
synchronicity like that left no room for doubt. When
I returned for my interview an hour later, I was hired
at once and told to report for work Monday morning.

The second incident to provide me with a reminder
of the powerful behind-the-scenes influence of the invisible world was far more dramatic than the first and

relates directly to this very spring beside which I now entertain the twilight's deepening. By the time of its occurrence, I had been working at the post office for two and a half years, during which Sherry and I had occupied our spare time researching various regions of the United States to determine the best areas to look for land.

We had subscribed to the National Weather Service's daily weather maps showing temperatures and amounts of precipitation throughout the country, and they had helped us zero in on regions of interest. The U.C. Berkeley Bancroft Library filled in additional details. We also kept up with current United and Strout farm catalogs, studying properties and prices and circling in our Rand McNally Road Atlas the towns where suitable land might be found.

Our primary criteria were cost, climate, and rainfall—in that order—but we also took into consideration factors such as population density, distance from nuclear power plants, proximity to the Amish, and the various regions' natural history and beauty. By the time of this second incident, we had concluded from our research that we wanted to buy a farm in the Missouri Ozarks. On our road atlas we had circled several dozen Ozark towns with real estate listings in our price range.

Since Sherry and I were equally passionate about pursuing this, our common goal, I had been able to do my part with a degree of discipline that would have been impossible without an equally dedicated partner. At the post office, I had worked all the overtime I could, often six days a week, and had not yet taken any of my annual leave, which I had allowed to accumulate.

We had managed our budget in a manner that, while forgoing no necessities, allowed us to save nearly a third of my salary. (Heating with wood, doing with-out electricity, buying healthful whole-grain foods in bulk, grinding our own wheat into flour, shopping in Salvation Army stores, growing a large garden, reduc-ing our rent by making repairs and improvements for our landlady—it was not as difficult as it may sound.) We actually lived well during those years, but our em-phasis was saving money to buy ourselves, as Paul Simon sings, "an acre of land, deep forest green"—more if it proved affordable.

When the dream came, we had fifty-five hundred dollars in the bank.

Although it wasn't actually a dream.

In the middle of the night I was awakened by a voice. It was the second of only three occasions in my life when in the absence of any identifiable speaker I heard audible words that sounded as though they were spoken directly in my ears. The words that awoke me were these—

It is the second day of the second month.

Possibly the voice had intended to say more. I will never know, because on hearing those words I sat bolt upright in bed, my heart racing, the only thought in my mind, *What the hell was that?*

I glanced at the clock. *Two* minutes after *two* A.M.

Sherry was sound asleep; the house was quiet. There was no one else in the room, no one around. I looked at the clock again and suddenly I shivered from head to toe. The hair literally rose on my skin. For when I looked at the clock that second time, it struck me like a thunderbolt—

This is the *second* minute of the *second* hour of the *second* day of the *second* month of the year. I had barely begun to digest this when I was hit with the aftershock of a follow-up realization: This was also the decade's *second* year.

I woke up Sherry.

Pointing half incoherently at the clock, I did my best to convey what had just happened. By the time I had finished my account and shared my initial impressions, she too was sitting bolt upright. After a few moments, she turned to me and speaking slowly said, "Ken . . . "

"What?"

"When this voice woke you, it said *It's the second day of the second month,* right? Then you noticed it was the second minute of the second hour, and figured out about the years and all?"

"Yeah, that's just how it went."

"And a minute ago you said that you thought the voice might have gone on to say more if you hadn't sat up and panicked like that—"

"It scared the hell out of me. I wish I hadn't reacted that way, but I did. It seemed that when I sat up so quickly and swore and everything, I sort of, you know, blew it away, whatever it was."

"Right. Well, I thought of a couple of things. I don't know if they're part of what the voice was about to say, but they might have something to do with it."

"What are they?" I asked.

"Well, I know this sounds kind of crazy, but the *second* half of this century is *twenty-two* years old; and what's really strange, your birthday is December first."

"What's my birthday got to do with anything?"

"I'm not sure, nothing maybe, but you're *twenty-two* years old, and your birthday was *two* months—"

"—and *two* days ago as of tomorrow! I hadn't thought of that!"

"Listen," she said, "I know this whole thing seems pretty weird—"

"No kidding."

"—but we've always said we believed in magic."

"Like the way I got my job at the post office?"

"Yeah, there's something like that behind this, too. I can feel it."

"I know, I feel it, too. But what does it mean?"

"Maybe there's something we're missing, something we're supposed to see, or understand."

"Or *do* maybe," I added thoughtfully.

"But what?"

"That's what we've got to find out."

We spent the next hour discussing the message and speculating on its meaning. After some quick calculating, I told her that as near as I could figure, such an unusual date involving the number two occurred only four times every thousand years. She pointed out that the number four was two squared, as well as a pair of twos added together. We knew it had to mean something, but our discussion was unable to shed any light on it. We finally drifted back to sleep with the meaning of the interrupted message still very much a mystery.

At work the next morning during my coffee break, I happened to pick up a copy of the *Wall Street Journal*. A front-page story leaped out at me—something about the dollar's rapid decline in value in relation to foreign currencies. The details are unimportant now, but if the article's forecast proved accurate, my intuition told me that rural land prices would soon soar. By the time I had finished reading the piece, I knew—with a sense of irrational yet thoroughly unshakable certainty—that I should immediately withdraw our savings, drive to the Ozarks, and purchase land.

There was no time for hesitation. After getting the approval of my immediate supervisor, George Banks, I went right to the postmaster's office and requested emergency annual leave. Since my unused leave had been accumulating during the entire two and a half years I had been employed as timekeeper—and since I told him truthfully that an urgent family matter had suddenly arisen—I had no problem in securing my requested two weeks' leave.

Next morning I gathered up our Strout and United real estate catalogs, Rand McNally Road Atlas, a thermos of coffee, and nearly a week's worth of food that Sherry had stayed up late packing for me.

I hugged her and the children good-bye, climbed in the truck, and headed for Missouri, never once questioning that it was the right thing to do. I knew that it was. Sherry? She was as certain of the appropriateness of this sudden venture as I was. Somehow, from within herself, she also knew. Physically I may have driven off alone, but she was with me every mile of the way, our spirits in total accord.

Mountain View, Missouri, lay roughly in the center of the Ozark towns that we had circled on our map. It had several interesting listings in our price range and had the added recommendation of being home to an Amish carpenter with whom I occasionally corresponded. Since I had less than a week before I would have to begin the long two-thousand-mile drive back, to make the most efficient use of my time, I decided that I would not begin looking for property until I had reached Mountain View. From its central location I could fan out to explore other areas with a minimum of unnecessary driving.

When I finally arrived in this central Ozark town of just over a thousand people, I pulled up outside the first real estate office I saw—the Lucille Sigler Agency, which was then situated in a small building on Highway 60 across from the St. Francis Hospital. Lucille herself was seated behind the desk as I entered and described the type of property I hoped to find.

"About eighty acres," I said, "preferably iso-lated—be great if it was at the end of a dirt road—not more than a third of the land cleared, mostly wooded." I went on to explain that while these were our most important criteria, it would be ideal if the property had an old house on it, nothing in too good condition because we needed to keep the price down, just something we could live in while we built. I also told her that while it was not essential, it would be a big plus for us if the property had a spring.

Without realizing it, I had described this land I am sitting on today. At first Lucille did not mention this farm. She read descriptions of a number of other listings, suggesting that we go look at each of them in turn. None of them sounded worth the time it would take to drive there. No problem, she said; she didn't mind driving. They were close by, twenty acres here on the road, forty acres off the road there. But none of them roused even the slightest flicker of my inter-est, and I remained adamant.

"I won't waste your time, Lucille. None of those properties sounds like what I'm looking for." I was getting up to leave when she paused thoughtfully and said, it seemed with some reluctance, "Wait. Don't go yet. I know of a place like the one you described. I've been thinking of it as we talked, but I didn't want to mention it because, well, it's not actually on the mar-ket yet.

"You see, my sister just called me last night and told me it looks as though she and her husband are going to be getting a divorce. They've got an old cabin back in the woods where they go on weekends sometimes, but with the divorce and all, she said they were thinking of putting it up for sale. It comes with

eighty acres, sits at the end of a dirt road, and I believe there's a spring on the property."

By then I was all ears. "Yes, definitely," I said.
"Let's go have a look at it."

"We can go right now if you want."

"Sounds good."

From Lucille's jeep I got my first glimpse of the
spectacularly beautiful Jacks Fork River. Soon after
crossing it, we left the state highway for a narrow
county road, which after a few miles of breathtaking
scenery we abandoned for a dirt road that in places
was hardly more than an overgrown deer trail. Head-
light-tall weeds grew down its center, and its generous litter of fallen branches suggested it had not been
traveled for several months.

When after a mile or so she pulled up into a yard
next to an old farmhouse, it all looked so familiar I
could hardly believe my eyes. As I stepped out of her
jeep—the very instant my feet hit the ground—I felt
an overwhelming rush of emotion, a powerful juxtaposition of joy and sorrow blended in a mixture so
deep and compelling that tears welled up behind my
eyes like floodwaters behind a straining dam.

My impression was one of profound personal acquaintance with this land, a sense that here a tremen-
dous amount of experience existed—for myself, my
family, maybe even future generations. I was filled
with an awareness of vast and intimate involvement
with this particular piece of ground, and, strangely
enough, not all of it pertained to the future—but that
is another story.

The moment I began to feel this, I had turned from
Lucille's jeep and started walking toward the forest in
hopes of concealing my increasingly watery eyes. But
I was barely holding my own. The first tear had escaped and begun its meander down my cheek—and I

was probably no more than a few seconds from a point when, back to her or no, the shaking of my shoulders would be a dead giveaway—when all at once I realized that crying at this particular moment would seriously jeopardize my bargaining position.

Repression is the quintessence of wisdom at times, and this was clearly one of them. Instantly I clicked into a horse-trading mode and began the expected, but wholly unnecessary, tour of the land, for I knew, of course, that I would buy it. And I did—that very day. I bought the first farm I looked at. And I never regretted it. But I've always had a kind of intuitive suspicion that some secret deal had been struck behind my back, that this forest here was actually the party who had paid the cash, and that I was the one bought and paid for.

Our fifty-five hundred dollars in savings covered all but two thousand dollars of the purchase price, which I had no problem borrowing from the bank. Two years later, before we had made any improvements (other than repairing the cistern and painting the farmhouse roof), I was offered nineteen thousand dollars for the property. Land prices in the Ozarks had doubled, and in some places tripled, during those two years.

Jessie and Patrick were born under the tin roof of that old farmhouse and had already logged in a few years by the time Lucille's sister and her husband finally stopped by one day to visit. Turns out they had never gotten a divorce.

"Wished we'd kept the place," Elmer told me.

These former owners were good folks, and we enjoyed our visit with them. From what I gathered, they had taken good care of the property during the years they held title, but my sympathy for their loss of stewardship was mitigated by the discovery that before putting the place on the market they had planned to harvest all the larger trees.

No blame. Just the way everyone used to do things back then; and in an economy as poor as the Ozarks, the sale of timber is often necessary just to keep in groceries. But I have wondered sometimes if the voice that awoke me from my sleep and precipitated my being in the right place at precisely the right time might have had something to do with this forest, these trees.

Time is a funny thing. Past and future may one day prove less rigid than we think. In light of my subsequent involvement with the intelligences that inhabit so many of this area's older trees, and our eventual establishment of a land trust to protect them, I've wondered if possibly some resident of that mysterious invisible world may have delivered that fateful February message on their behalf, a plea— perhaps from a particular tree.

I give the thought a moment to sink in. It would make sense. The oldest and largest tree within sight of the basin here is an oak that grows where the ledge above me merges into the hillside. As I look out from beneath the ledge I can see its lower branches hanging motionless in the twilight. It occurs to me that I have been sitting beneath it all this while. In fact its roots are nearly over my head. Through all the long years of this century, and for the better part of the last, this tree has grown directly above the spring, sheltering the spot where the springwater emerges from beneath the forest, from beneath our home and garden, to splash, as it splashes in front of me now, upon the basin's limestone floor.

A slight tremor ripples through its leaves.

There is no wind.

STANDING, REFRESHED FROM ONE last, long draft
of the cool springwater, I lift my eyes to the old oak
that grows above the ledge I had been sitting beneath. While its leaves remain motionless, I study the
old tree for a moment, wondering. But a robin seems
reluctant to have her evening drink while I remain, so
I will defer to her and to the other creatures who seek
refreshment here and go about my way.

Climbing out of the spring basin into the open
world above, the sounds of splashing water and of
countless chirping frogs recede. For the first time I
notice how still the evening has become; it is quiet
here, slightly brighter, and the air, not so cool as
below.

The planet's gentle spin has long obscured the sun
behind the wooded hills to the west. Yet, as if reluctant to part from so fair a land, a thin band of sunlight still catches the uppermost leaves of the trees
that ride the highest elevation of the eastern ridge—a
lingering ribbon of day that even as I watch shimmers
a final farewell and floats upward, yielding to the
night's deepening shadow. Far above, still enjoying
the light of a sun that has left the world below, a lone
hawk glides effortlessly upon some invisible current,
her wings perfectly still. Could it be the same goshawk
I so admired before? She flies too high to be sure.

> *How do you know but ev'ry Bird that cuts*
> *the airy way,*
> *Is an immense world of delight, clos'd*
> *by your senses five?*

I have no evidence that would convince another, but my soul answers Blake's question tonight as I watch this wondrous bird in flight. I know. Her world of delight is apparent as she spirals ever higher to catch the last of the setting sun's light.

Why are we so hesitant to credit animals with aesthetic sense? I have observed their ways for many years now, and I know they appreciate beauty. In fact I'm convinced that it motivates many creatures nearly as much as hunger or thirst.

During one summer we lived in Ireland, on days when the weather was clear, I would often go to a favorite spot. Hidden in a niche of a west-facing cliff high above the sea, I would sit on a sheltered rock, out of the wind, where I could enjoy an unobstructed view of the sun as it disappeared into the Atlantic.

Twenty feet directly below my seat—before the cliff continued the remainder of its hundred-foot plunge toward the breakers below—a projection of grassy rock appeared to hover miraculously between sea and sky. There, every evening on that green peninsula above the waves, a delegation of the many rabbits who populated burrows throughout the cliff would come, often side by side with their mates, to sit and enjoy the sunset. I have watched rabbits sitting motionless there for nearly an hour, staring out to sea, appreciating the sunsets in a way so similar to my own that our rapport became as deep as any I have experienced with a cat on my lap before the fire or a dog sitting at my side gazing as intently as I into the flames.

Cows, too, I have noticed, appreciate beauty—and perhaps a good deal more than many humans. For fourteen of these last twenty years, we have kept a milk cow, sometimes two. I have grown close to several in that time, but I remember old Bossie, our yellow Guernsey, the best. Often I would watch a sunset from the roof of the barn while she watched from her vantage below, our eyes fixed on the same sunset-colored clouds, our minds contemplating, it seemed, the same eternal mysteries.

Shouldering my backpack in preparation for the journey home, I lean forward a moment, lowering my eyes to the base of the hill that rises steeply to the north. I pause, puzzled, then step back for a better look. How differently everything appears in these murky, late twilight shadows. Even things with which I thought myself familiar reveal uncanny depths that I had not noticed before.

Several large volcanic blocks suddenly seem out of place. Their bubbly, pockmarked surfaces appear somehow incongruous where they rest among the smoother stone typical of this stratum. Near-rectangular blocks of both types of stone seem to form an artificial ledge here, a long, low shelf along the base of the hill.

Looking upward, the source of the volcanic rock is plain: It came from an exposed stratum higher up the hillside. What are they doing down here, these large five- and six-hundred-pound blocks, arranged alongside blocks of limestone in—

Could they form the bed of an old road? Climbing up to have a look, I brush aside the leaves and find smaller rocks arranged above them in Roman fashion, and above them, smaller rocks, then gravel, clay, and perhaps a half century of leaf mold. As I stand

and look off into the forest, my perspective suddenly shifts as it does when discovering a hidden picture in a child's puzzle. I am standing in the middle of an overgrown throughway.

Despite the maple saplings and massive yucca plant now growing in its center, I can easily make out its former course. This is, after all, the logical place to cross the creek. The old roadway hugs the base of the hillside, taking advantage of natural features, but this stretch here where the hill is too steep to permit passage otherwise had to be deliberately built up, which explains the telltale rearrangement of volcanic block.

This is no Indian trail, of course, but an early settlers' road, built most likely by those who secured homestead grants to this land in the 1850s and 1860s and who no doubt depended on this spring for their drinking water. Where the road once came out above the midlands pool, it must have been a bumpy ride across the uneven rocks for an old wagon with no rubber on its tires; but at least here a crossing was possible.

Examining the rocks, I look for evidence of old wheel tracks. Strange to think of there once having been a road down here; it is now such a quiet, out-of-the-way spot. But there was a time before the Great Depression when the population of these hills reached a peak considerably greater than today's, and it is said that the main road from Summersville to Birch Tree once ran through here, although until now I was never sure just where it had crossed this creek. I would stay and listen for phantom stages passing in the dusk, but the evening magic calls me onward.

A deep stillness now hangs almost like liquid in the air, and I feel myself drawn toward the warm darkness below the arching foliage where the path begins its meandering homeward way.

Preparing to leave this area that has given me so much today, I am reminded of a custom they have in Japan. After a meeting, or *gosshuku*, as one is leaving the room, one turns, places hands together, and bows toward the room, thanking it for having provided its space. I have seen this gesture, this appreciative acknowledgment of space, many times upon leaving rooms in Japan. I have seen even ticket collectors and vendors on Tokyo's trains bow as they leave the cars. Something in my soul caught the cultural wisdom behind this gesture of respect, and I cannot leave the spring today without extending a brief but heartfelt thank you.

It rarely occurs to me to do this after something as routine as jogging, but Sherry never forgets. Each day after her run she turns, bows briefly, and thanks the forest. Today I do the same. It helps to assuage the reluctance I feel to leave here and return to my familiar world—though how familiar it will be after today is a good question. I carry with me something I did not have this morning.

It came as no great revelation or dramatic insight. Just a simple reminder that I chose my responsibilities and that behind each of them is love. They are not burdens or chores; they are expressions of love. When I am not caught up in anxiety, I enjoy the activities they require. And of all my chosen tasks and commitments, those that bring the greatest challenges, frustrations, joy, and satisfaction are those that are born of my deepest love, my love for those who depend on my labor. As my preoccupations and concerns have receded in the course of this day, that love has emerged paramount. Far from dreading going back to my daily sphere, my office and all that awaits me there, I now feel eager to return and take a fresh look at things. With a renewed sense of humor and perspective.

My course now leads me into shadow. Around the dogwoods, sassafras, and young oaks that flank the path, grape, morning glory, and ivy vines spiral upward, interlacing overhead into a natural pergola that marks the beginning of my winding path home. I move quietly, making as little noise as possible.

Turkeys often roost along this hillside in the evening, and I have come to feel almost as protective for their nests among the leaves of the forest's floor as the mother hens themselves. More than once this time of day I have inadvertently frightened one of the large, ungainly birds; it makes a powerful racket as it explodes out of the brush and flies noisily into the trees.

Wild turkeys are a strange lot. The weaving, swaying motion of their long, slender necks appears more serpentine than birdlike, and like many of the larger birds, they exhibit a reluctance to fly. Nearly every day for several years we would see a flock of fourteen full-grown turkeys and an attending entourage of chicks out in the pasture beyond our garden fence. Early in the morning and during the evening twilight, we would watch them from our kitchen window. It seemed they preferred these dimly-lit hours for venturing near our house and garden.

One evening I cautiously stepped outside, allowing them to see me. We had been observing them for weeks, careful when they were near not to slam doors or make loud noises that might frighten them away. The time had come to let them know that we did not pose a threat. I stood in full view for a minute, then went quietly back inside, repeating this every day for the next few weeks. Gradually it had its effect. The turkeys came nearer and nearer to the house, even during the day. As the months passed and the summer grew increasingly dry, their foraging became more difficult. By then they knew that we were not going to harm them, so, noticing things to eat closer to our house, they became quite bold.

Looking out the window one morning I saw the whole flock right in our front yard, not ten feet from our kitchen window. And in the center of the flock, surrounded by gobblers larger than he was, toddled our fourteen-month-old son, Patrick.

The turkeys circled around him, eying him warily, first from one eye and then from the other, as if they couldn't quite believe what they saw. Inquisitively they wove their long necks back and forth, studying the toddler, apparently trying to place him in some category, some familiar niche of their turkey worldview.

Gradually they seemed to conclude that this newest addition to their numbers was not even a bird, much less a turkey, and slowly they began edging away. Patrick learned a new word that day: *gurkey*. Every bird he saw, even years after that, whether cardinal, finch, sparrow, or jay, he called a gurkey. And I suspect the turkeys, too, might have learned something: that humans really are creatures, after all, strange ones to be sure, but maybe not so incomprehensible as they had once supposed.

Tonight I have succeeded in not disturbing these feathered foragers that, had it been left to Benjamin Franklin, would have become America's national bird. I am past their nesting grounds, and all is well.

The moon, which will be full tonight, has not yet risen. Even after its rising it will take some time for its light to reach this point where my path passes

through the First Rocks, and where I can't help but
linger a while. Above, the first stars shine, while on a
nearby branch a whippoorwill repeats her age-old
song. Suddenly she stops, and I catch a glimpse of her
flitting ghostlike among the trees.

Whippoorwills come to life at dawn and dusk.
They are not shy of human company, these seldom-
seen but often-heard birds. They appreciate a human
audience, often fluttering silently to the ground
within a few feet of our porch and directing their serenades in our direction. Not conspicuous birds to
begin with, one rarely notices them in the summer,
though on cool nights their song can be heard off in
the woods. We hear them most often in late spring
and early summer—and then only near dawn or
dusk. Just as geese herald the coming of spring, whippoorwills herald the arrival of summer. Hearing that
first whippoorwill off in the woods on a warm spring
evening will always bring us into the yard to listen. It
is a sure and welcome sign that summer is near.

Although it's usually a ground-nesting bird, one
young whippoorwill somehow got it into her head,
during our first season in the long-vacant farmhouse,
to nest beneath the tin immediately above our bedroom window. Like an alarm clock she would go off
punctually at five o'clock each morning and would
not stop until the sun was up.

Unable to sleep during those long, monotonous
predawn serenades, I eventually ran out of things to
do. To pass the time I made a game of counting how
many "whippoorwill, whippoorwill" sequences the
tireless little chanter could produce before finally
pausing for an all-too-brief rest. Thirty-seven was
her record. It was a lot to put up with that year, but
I never found it in me to chase that little bird and

her young family away. They nested with us all that season.

Leaving the First Rocks, it is already too dark to see the path before me, but overhead, stars shining between the treetops show its course. Even on nights when the stars are obscured by clouds, my feet have no trouble sensing the absence of leaves that distinguishes path from forest.

We lived here for nearly a decade without owning a flashlight. It wasn't until we began noticing our visitors stumbling around in the dark that we realized there was anything unusual in this. Our children regularly played outside after dark; they were notorious for their high-speed chases among the trees. Having no difficulty getting around myself, I never thought to question them on their own means of navigation. But every now and then they would claim to have seen an unexplained light or some glowing object weaving in and out among the trees, and about these I did occasionally question them.

One moonless night when a half dozen youngsters rushed excitedly into the house to tell me of a strange, glowing shape they had just seen, I separated two of them: our daughter, Becky, and Dawn, a girl who boarded with us during school term. I sat them down in separate rooms, gave them pencil and paper, and asked them each to draw me a picture of it. Their finished drawings were conceptually identical—two glowing circles connected by a long, thin, luminous fiber.

Questioned separately, they complemented their illustrations with verbal accounts in which I found no discrepancies. The creature, they said, moved through the forest like an animal but made no sound. Neither they nor the other children showed any fear of it. In fact they were disappointed that it hadn't stayed longer.

Behind me, in the direction of the spring, the booming voice of a barred owl breaks the silence with a long, inquisitive *who-who-who-whooooooo,* which leaves an eerie echo bouncing among the hills. Even before the echo has died, it is answered by the hoot of another owl off to the west. The first owl hoots again from the spring, and the western owl replies in an excited, somewhat frenzied tone. The exchange is repeated several times, but while one owl's excitement grows, the other owl seems to grow more tentative, even a little cautious.

From the surrounding area other owls join in, each successive hoot coming from a location nearer and nearer to the spring. For a few gloriously cacophonous seconds they all converge, and it sounds as though a whole parliament were deeply embroiled in some passionate debate. Abruptly they stop. The night absorbs a final echo, and silence once more reigns beneath the trees.

These barred owls are among my favorite birds. Their hoots can be heard for up to four or five miles on a still night, which, not surprisingly, is when they most enjoy conversing in their deep, reverberating tones. Often on a still night I will imitate their call—one of the few bird calls I can duplicate with relative accuracy. Without fail, one will answer from off in the distance, sometimes several, drawing closer as I repeat the call.

My brother, Tom, also does a convincing owl imitation. Some nights, from his home across the hollow, he tries to fool me with his hoots, and usually I play along. We learned the barred owl's call from our father, who once belonged to a fraternity of some sort that used it as their rallying cry.

When I was a boy, and my father was still in his twenties, I remember walking out on the street with him on one of those immaculately still Chicago winter nights when the frozen, snow-covered ground enabled the slam of a car door to be heard a mile and a half away. Dad let rip with a hair-raising hoot, then dropped silent. A few seconds later, away off in the distance, we heard someone hooting back in similar fashion . . . or was it an owl?

Tom and I never got all the details on just what kind of gang or club our father was involved in (and it may be just as well that we didn't), but the owl hoot stuck with us. The first time we heard the owls here in Missouri, we both got chills, imagining our father, long deceased, signaling to us across the years from another still, snow-covered winter's night.

Coming home late a few weeks ago, my headlights fell on a baby barred owl drinking from a puddle in the middle of the road. He froze, blinded by the unexpected light. Ever since reading Farley Mowat's *Owls in the Family*, I had been hoping for an opportunity to befriend a baby owl; so I opened the door of the truck quietly and eased my way toward him. I approached to within a foot of the little bird before he finally flew off into the bushes.

Many nights near that same dip in the road I have seen owls, sometimes in flight, but usually resting in the lower branches of a tree. In the old days a place would often acquire its name from such frequent animal visitors. A low spot like that where the road crosses the hollow would probably once have been named Owl Hollow. Native Americans and settlers alike named places after the creatures who frequented

them. Bear Ridge and Panther Springs lie just a few
miles south of here. But there are many: Owl's Bend,
Deer Lick, Eagle Rock, Bull Shoals, Wolf Pen, Buf-
falo River, Beaver Creek.

These place names are understandable. All of these
animals are, or were recently, associated with these
spots. But there is a place I wonder about, just across
the river from our farm: Angel Ridge. How it got that
name I am not sure, but there have been winter
nights when I have heard calls from beings who may
very well deserve that appellation.

As my path takes me from the hollow's level
ground, and I follow its northward curve up the hill
toward home, to say that I am actually *seeing* would
be misleading, but I have no trouble finding my way.
Objects possess an inner glow that one can learn to
sense if able to suspend the natural preference for lu-
mens. This subtle effervescence would probably not
register on the visible light spectrum, though it may
be related in some way to those glowing fields that
show up in Kirlian photography.

On a recent tour of nearby Round Spring Cave,
when we had reached the deepest cavern, a half mile
beneath the surface of the earth, the park guide had
us all sit down and turn out our flashlights while she
pointed out what "true blackness" was and how
rarely people ever experienced such a total absence of
light.

"Pass your hand in front of your face," she suggested. "You can't see anything, can you?"

Moving my hand before my eyes, I saw the movement as a lightly glowing blur. While she was telling
us we could not see, I repeated the gesture several
times, seeing the same faintly glowing blur each time
my hand passed before me. Wondering if I would ex-

perience the same effect, I repeated the gesture with my eyes closed. Sure enough, I could still detect the same faint glow of movement. The perception apparently had nothing to do with my eyes.

Although I am now able vaguely to distinguish a few of the general features of these surroundings with my eyes closed, I am not yet familiar enough with the odd nuances of this metavisual sense to trust it while moving about among so many trees. With sufficient practice I suppose one could get used to that sense, whatever it is.

Perception takes many forms. My feet *feel* the path beneath them, which already has taken me well up the hill. When my ears *hear* the crackle of leaves or the snapping of twigs, the sound lets me know I have left it and stepped off into the forest. On the path, passage is silent. Off the path, one's movements are loud and disruptive and often attract unwanted attention.

Attention. My own is drawn by a firelike flickering from the direction I have just come. Turning, I see an orange glow among the ridge-top trees a mile to the east. My climb up the hill has brought me to an elevation a hundred or more feet above the spring, to a steep and grassy slope where no trees obstruct my view. The orange glow looks nearly like a signal fire there atop the distant ridge. Between it and the starlight there is now light enough to look out above the hollow, across the tops of the trees beneath which I spent my day.

I take a seat in the grass, and for a long while I rest beyond thought, wordlessly contemplating the silent rising of the moon. Full moon. Planting moon. Moon when the Rivers Warm.

The earth's natural satellite appears to shrink as it floats slowly upward through the trees. By the time it clears the ridge, the lower atmosphere has released its magnifying spell, and as its ascent continues into the starry constellations of our northern sky, its orangy color yields to the crisp clarity of white. I can see now nearly as well as in daylight, but the quality of the light and my impressions of what it reveals are markedly different from sunlit hours.

There is a dimension apparent by moonlight not revealed by day. While sunlight permits only shade of its own making, the moon is more generous, opening her shadows to all. Her softer rays seem to evoke the essences of things, and one can sometimes see them, or imagine one does, at play—as if shy and subtle entities, intimidated by too-brilliant definition, emerge from certain forest life-forms on nights like this to enjoy the light of the moon.

Rising to embark on the final leg of my journey, I hear not a sound, not an owl or a whippoorwill, not a breath of wind to stir the leaves. In the silent stillness, the moon's light appears to come from everywhere, from within the things I pass. Every angle, every variation of its soft, falling-like-rain rays, emphasizes distinct features of the landscape.

Lamplights of buttercups illuminate the sides of the path, each a glowing phosphorescence in the diffused light of the rising lunar world.

Tree trunks glide by as slowly I walk past, and for a moment it seems they are dancing beside me on the hillside. There is a greater variety of trees up here where the night's temperatures remain warmer than down in the hollow: more walnut, cedar, black locust, wild cherry, plum, pear. Oaks and hickories still dominate, but here, unlike below, there are still a few surviving virgin pine. Tonight these trees, these beings of the hills, feel almost like people, hill beings, celebrating their chosen spots upon this rock-strewn slope. Stationary when I am stationary, appearing to move when I move. In reality they are indeed mobile creatures, as anyone who has ever seen an oak topple a wall knows only too well.

Trees are neither fleeting dots nor enduring lines, but dashes in the language of eternity. Duration moves in their leaves, lives, breathes. Birds nest in them. People make homes of them. Their time is slower than our human time, yet in their own lives they are no less passionately alive. Treeing before me in the moonlight, this ancient hillside transmutes its limestone into living wood, and through its trees, reaches upward to embrace the stars.

In her trees earth mingles with sun, and sun with earth. What makes a leaf? What makes the needle of a pine? What makes the acorn? The fir cone? The flower of the oak? Are they not, when all is said and done, a union of the stardust that is earth—and the starlight of the sun?

We come here, all of us, seeking a balance between energy and form, spirit and matter, between this sunlight and this clay. Trees find that balance in wooden rings, rough bark, green leaves, needles, cones, roots, and foliage. The birds find their balance suspended in air. Star and stone. We blend them our way, they blend them theirs. And while tonight these trees may dance to a slower drum than I, my spirit hears a drum slower still.

I think back to that surveyor's remark. Deep in some unnamed recess of my soul, somewhere in that ocean of being that splashes upward to form this wave, this life that tonight I am, a part of me remembers these hills when they were dressed in virgin pine. And before, those eons before this creek was ocean floor, when the ancient Francois range rose young, jagged, craggy as the Himalayas, when silvery snows filled its valleys, and across the snow volcanic carpets of molten lava rolled. And later, too, that part of me stood watch when the earth rumbled and thrust this land again into the sky.

We have journeyed long and far—spirits in this material world.

Yet before and after this terrestrial biology, we are spirits, you and I. Longing for structures that would last for more than a moment, for more than an hour or a day, we came here to experience this warm and fertile world, to play upon its surface, to partake of it through forms of living clay. Some of us touch the earth through human forms, some through the forms of the owls and whippoorwills who fly these moonlit skies. Some of us swim as salmon in her streams or leap as dolphins in her seas. Some of us wear the fur of the four-footed and sniff the shifting of the ageless winds. And some of us, some of us express ourselves in the stately dances of these trees. I recognize them in the moon's soft light, these friends, old friends from before.

I wear these human cells today, these clothes upon my back. I am glad for them, I care for them, I keep them from harm's way. But I remove them at the end of the day. I have many suits, this human dress but one. Like you. Like these trees. Like the owl now calling—to me, it seems—across these ancient, moonlit hills.

For information on Ken Carey's workshops and speaking engagements, write to Starseed Seminars, Star Route Box 70, Mountain View, Missouri 65548.

Praise for Ken Carey's *Flat Rock Journal*

"Ken Carey is the rare breed of an environment-alistwho doesn't write like one. Unlike the heavy-handedness of the Thou-shalt-not-pollute school, Carey, like Robert Frost, instead reminds us of the joy to be found in a closer look at the earth."
—*The Grand Rapids Cadence*

"A pine tree provides a vision of loggers, a raven ex-plains bird consciousness. . . . At the heart of *Flat Rock Journal* is one man's reverence for the miracu-lous nature of life, a reverence that flows as sweet and clear as the Ozark spring water he so lovingly de-scribes."—*Los Angeles Times*

"A swirling dance of spirit and nature told with ex-traordinary awareness, wit, and insight . . . a beauti-ful addition to the finest of American nature writing."—*Magical Blend Magazine*

"*Flat Rock Journal* should inspire others to look closely at their own ties to natural communities."
—*St. Louis Post-Dispatch*

"An always engaging memoir . . . in the spirit of Henry David Thoreau—and of William Shake-speare."—*Chronicles Magazine*

"[Carey] sees life as a cross-species experience to be shared by those who can shed their material form—a thought not distant from Emerson's transcendental Oversoul. . . . [He] describes a mating romance among a trio of five-inch lizards as a battle of the dinosaurs not unlike the battle of the ants in *Walden*. . . . Most delightful is Carey's whistling a ditty from Handel to a pond of singing frogs, then a little Led Zeppelin and a few Grateful Dead riffs."
—*Kirkus Reviews*

"This charming memoir reflects Carey's love of nature and his commitment to preserving the environment."—*Publishers Weekly*

"Ken Carey has the Irishman's skill, humor, and grace in telling stories; his stories give a world Occam's razor never sliced: a tumble of beauty, magic, and 'metavision.' And who is to say his is not as true as the world many of the rest of us live in more regularly? The chapter on frogs, alone, is worth the price of admission."—Sue Hubbell, author of *Broadsides from the Other Orders*

"[Carey] like John Muir likes nothing better than riding out a storm while perched high in the branches of a tree."—*The Hartford Courant*

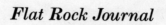

Flat Rock Journal

ALSO BY KEN CAREY

The Third Millennium
The Starseed Transmissions
Vision
Return of the Bird Tribes

Flat Rock Journal

A Day in the Ozark Mountains

Ken Carey

HarperSanFrancisco
A Division of HarperCollins*Publishers*

HarperSanFrancisco and the authors, in association with the Rainforest Action Network, will facilitate the planting of two trees for every one tree used in the manufacture of this book.

Text design and illustration by Eric Holub

FIRST HARPERCOLLINS PAPERBACK EDITION PUBLISHED IN 1995

Library of Congress Cataloging-in-Publication Data
Carey, Ken.
Flat rock journal : a day in the Ozark Mountains / Ken Carey. —
1st ed.
p.   cm.
ISBN 0–06–251006–1 (cloth : alk. paper)
ISBN 0–06–250275–1 (pbk. : alk. paper)
1. Ozark Mountains—Description and travel.   2. Natural
history—Ozark Mountains.   3. Carey, Ken—Homes and
haunts—Ozark Mountains.   I. Title.
F472.09C37   1993
917.67'1—dc20   92–53059
CIP

95 96 97 98 99 ❖ HAD 10 9 8 7 6 5 4 3 2 1